COUNTRY PADRE

Country Padre

by PHILIP WRIGHT, MBE

EGON PUBLISHERS LTD
Meeting House Lane, Church Street,
Baldock, Herts. SG7 5BP

First published in 1980
by Egon Publishers, Ltd.
Meeting House Lane, Church Street, Baldock, Herts.
Revised Edition 1981

Copyright © Egon Publishers Ltd.
and Philip Wright

ISBN 0 905858 13 1

Bookjacket photography by Tony Tween

Typesetting and design by
Art Anonymous, Biggleswade, Beds.

Printed in England by
S. G. Street & Co. Ltd
Meeting House Lane, Church Street,
Baldock, Herts. SG7 5BP

DEDICATION

*To all who have helped me on life's pilgrimage
particularly my family and friends.*

ACKNOWLEDGEMENTS

I would like to thank Mrs. Davinda Maimi for typing the Ms; and Mrs. Ann Cunningham for reading same.

My thanks are also due to the following who have provided photographs: Ray Horsnall, Peter Russell, Geoff Baker, Ron Goose, Maurice Nicholls Tony Ray, Barry Finch, Maurice Wright and Stan Peck. The other pictures are from my own camera.

Finally I wish to thank Egon Publishers Ltd for their kindly and personal help in producing the book.

PHILIP WRIGHT.

Queen Anne Cottage,
Greensted,
Ongar, Essex.

Chapter 1

The year 1908 was not particularly a vintage year in British history except for the fact that it was the year in which Lloyd George brought in old age pensions and was thereafter honoured by old fashioned country folk, years afterwards, referring to the pension as "Lloyd George". However, on 4th June that year I was born at Butler's Hall Farm, Hawstead which, like so many Suffolk farms, stands in more than one parish: Hawstead, Whepstead and Lawshall with the Boundary stone standing near the farmhouse gate. My sister Mary (Molly) had preceded me by eighteen months and my brother Maurice arrived five years after me.

Early recollections are hazy. I remember being weighed on a steelyard in the kitchen suspended from the ceiling. I also recall being pushed down Folly Lane in a pram. Folly Lane then was overgrown with grass but today is a tarred roadway. In this lane we visited imaginary Pixie folk whom we thought lived in the ditches and gullies among the ragwort and ladies hair grasses.

My father was of the old farming school — the mechanical era had not dawned. As a lad he had driven the horses which powered a threshing drum. This horse-drum came midway between the flail and the steam-driven threshing machine. Many of his workmen could use a flail and all of them could swing a scythe in the cornfield.

My father was born at the Church Farm, Bradfield Combust. Thus it came about that my father's early years were spent round and about Bradfield Hall, where the celebrated Arthur Young had made some 3,000 farming experiments and before reaching the age of 50 had surveyed 7,000 miles of British Agriculture. Arthur Young left the world richer by 240 volumes, which he had written or edited, upon Farming and Rural Economy.

Arthur Young was the first secretary of the newly formed Board of Agriculture and a personal friend of King George IV known to many as "Farmer" George. In my father's day the Rector of Bradfield was John Young, descendant of Arthur Young whose tomb is in Bradfield Churchyard.

Foot and mouth disease was not known then as a notifiable disease and did not involve the present day wholesale slaughter. My grandpa once dealt with an outbreak in a bunch of bullocks by isolating them in a meadow and treating their mouths with saltpetre and their feet with Stockholm tar. They went on to make capital butcher's beasts. I thought of this recently when I asked an old man what his new Vicar was like. He replied: "I reckon he's got foot and mouth disease".

"How's that?" I asked.

"Well, Philip, he can't preach and he 'ont visit!".

My grandpa held the additional position of "Road Surveyor" for the parish. These were usually farmers who were responsible for the upkeep of the roadways. Hand-picked stones from the land were carted on to the roads and his old account-books made fascinating reading.

My mother's maiden name was Honeywood. She was the eldest girl in a family of thirteen. They were a strong free-church family and in their very early years my grandparents on her side had a tough struggle. Grandad had been a working foreman at Foxearth, Essex and then at Rowhedge, Long Melford. He then risked taking over Rivetts Hall Farm, Hartest. When quite small I would stay there with them and with a bevy of aunts and uncles to fuss over me. I would travel there the five miles on "Lottie" a small tricycle with solid tyres propelled by pedals on the front wheel — no such thing as a chain nor intermittent gearing. Rivetts was a lovely 16th century farmhouse standing in a meadow with no roadway whatsoever leading to it.

The only car I ever saw there was a 1906 Belsize belonging to my uncle, John Honeywood. Pony-traps and cycles were the only other transports. Rivetts had graceful gables and a massive chimney-stack. A spiral staircase led to attics. Lead-framed windows had only just been replaced and in the back house was an open fireplace overhung by a spit and a hake. There was also the brick-oven in which Granny baked a week's supply of bread at one baking. The oak-panelled parlour with its richly carved over mantle was quite unique and the date 1594 was carved on the deeds, the room being completely oak-panelled. Scarcely two panels were the same size and there was a secret cupboard. On the wall hung a charter dated 1801 which granted the use of the room for religious meetings to a yeoman farmer named Benjamin Jennings.

A moat partially surrounded the house and I fished in the neighbouring pond but have never fished since. In comparatively recent years this lovely house was demolished by the Iveagh trust as it was in the part of the Chadacre estate farmed by the Agricultural Institute. If only they had made Rivetts the Principal's house and made a roadway to it, this lovely bit of old England could have been saved. Not so long ago I went up to the site and not a tile remains. Nothing but memories! When staying at Rivetts, I attended with my aunts and uncles the Gospel room at Hartest. We listened to long sermons and sung Sankey's hymns. My aunts would tease me by teaching very sad verses. "Little Jim" began:

> *"The Cottage was a thatched one,*
> *The outside small and mean,*
> *Yet everything beneath that cot*
> *Was wondrous, neat and clean.*
>
> *The night was dark and stormy,*
> *The wind was howling wild,*
> *A patient mother knelt beside*
> *The deathbed of her child . . . "*

Another poem began:

> *"Billy's dead and gone to glory,*
> *So is Billy's sister Nell . . . "*

Once more I would sob and beg them to stop!

But to return to early home life at Butler's Hall, I probably was as mischievous as most boys and have always had a sensitive, cowardly streak. Before 1914 a farm labourer's wage was often the price of a coomb of wheat. They were paid 12/- a week with two or three shillings extra for a horseman or cowman. Working hours were from 6 a.m. to 6 p.m. and perks were sometimes provided consisting of a rent free cottage, milk, and land in a field on which to grow their own potatoes. Harvest was 'taken' by piece work for an agreed sum and haytime and chopping-out mangolds was a means of earning a bit extra. I recall when 'paper money' replaced the golden sovereign and half sovereign my father's labourers refused to accept it.

"I ain't working damned hard for a bit of paper, not nohow". The poor old boys soon found it was "Hobson's Choice" — the treasury-note or nothing!

My mother introduced me to God quite soon and I cannot remember ever doubting that I was a child of His care. Neither can I recall a time when I failed to say my prayers. When my brother Maurice was born, mother was again (as had been the case of myself and sister) attended by Doctor

The Author at Hawstead village school with his brother and sister, 1917.

J. S. Hinnell who came from Bury St. Edmunds in a pony trap. There was no such thing as a maternity ward. My sister Molly was so annoyed at the birth of my brother Maurice that she threatened to drown him in the horsepond. However, he very soon came to be accepted into our small circle.

We began school at Whepstead, trudging the 1½ miles each way. Molly invariably stalked on in front. I loitered. We took our dinners in a covered basket and I still have that basket today.

Mr. and Mrs. Harry Phillips were heads of the school, and I recall the assemblies at which we sang lustily, "Oh it will be joyful, joyful, joyful, joyful . . . when we meet to part no more."

Phillips was in demand when farmers wanted stacks or root clamps measured or a field measured by the chain. The schoolmaster's figures were trusted for their accuracy. Debenham's threshing machine drawn by a Burrell engine would come to thresh the stacks and occasionally a set of Fowler steam ploughs would come after harvest to plough some of our Suffolk clay, for ours was heavy land indeed. I recall the engine drivers wearing a 1½ inch collar with a patent leather finish and black and white vertical stripes and quite washable. This was in contrast to the red and white spotted neckerchiefs favoured by most farm workers in those days, and which were also used for taking the ploughman's lunch into the fields.

We obtained our water from a deep well at Butler's Hall and over it was built a windlass for lowering the empty bucket and pulling it up, full. If a bucket was lost down below 'Creepers' would be affixed to the chain. These were upturned hooks which would catch the handle of the missing bucket and allow it to be wound-up on the handle. Water butts and tanks were used to catch rain-water from the house and buildings and this 'soft' water was used for washing, bathing and washing clothes.

As at most houses in the country at that time the sanitary arrangements were primitive. In the back garden was a little 'house', variously called the privy, the petty or the closet (there were other, rather more rude, names). Usually there was a two-holed seat to accommodate two adults at once!

Alongside would be a tiny "Dickie" seat for a child. The designers seemed to plan for communal sessions. At the receiving end was a vault which was cleared now and then and the contents carted to the fields for manure by horse and tumbril — I have done the job so I know first hand. Many folk were, however, replacing the vault by a large bucket.

My father was a long serving member of the Bury St. Edmunds Board of Guardians and of the Thingoe Rural District Council. At a very early age I used to read the agendas and reports for the monthly meetings. I recall that the Sanitary Inspector's name was Russell G. Saint and his job certainly must have demanded the 'Patience of a Saint'. People were not always in a nice, tractable mood when he called to enforce a council regulation. Reports would cover the disinfection of drains, fumigation of cottages after scarlet-fever and diptheria and also a list each month of "Privies converted into pail closets".

The story was told of an old man selling his cottage to go to live with his daughter. He was showing a young couple the Privy and they commented that there was no lock on the door. "Bless my soul and body" he exclaimed, "I've lived here sixty-five year and niver had a bucket pinched yet."

Damage by misfortune, i.e. fire, theft or flood, would partly be met by a "Brief" headed by the squire and parson. A sheet of paper would be taken from the church after the announcement, and sent round the parish for subscriptions for the unfortunate person or household. Old Mingay who lived on Straight Road, Whepstead was a 'Cobbler' who mended our boots. He not only soled and heeled them; he would *partly* sole them if they were not too bad, and this was called "Clumping". Always there were hobnails, steel toe-caps and heel-irons which were fitted afterwards.

The traditional farm-worker's smock was becoming less common in favour of a sleeved waistcoat with velvet front and a poacher's pocket. This would be worn with corduroy trousers and leather or cloth buskins. The jacket came well up to the neck, fastened with horse-shoe buttons. Nearly all of them had an inside poacher's pocket and even today, at seventy-two, all my jackets have a poacher's pocket and a buttonhole. The trousers had full-fronts which let down in front like a sailors. A fly front was scorned!

Old time editions of Kelly's directories always gave a list of 'Carriers' carts and their routes and destinations. The hostelry in Bury St. Edmunds, where they put-up, was also mentioned. One such carrier was a man named Clarke who drove from Melpost Hawstead via Whepstead to Bury every Saturday and Wednesday. Passengers and goods were conveyed in a four-wheeled, horse-drawn waggonette. He would also shop for people and chase over the town for their requirements for about tuppence. This, of course, was the forerunner of the country bus.

Mrs. Greenwood of Rowney Cottage used to help mother on washing days and we loved the old lady, who also made rag rugs. A washed sack would be taken apart, the sides and ends were bound and biased to prevent fraying. Mixed rags would be cut into strips four inches long by one inch wide, from any available material. These rag rugs were really beautiful. The rags were pegged in with a big steel bodkin. They took a long time to make but they lasted for years. In 1954, when I became Vicar of Woodford Bridge, I found two dear old sisters making these self-same rugs for the Church "Sale of Work" and we had one of their rugs for years. Miss Freestone and Mrs. Fogg were their names.

I re-visited Whepstead School a few years back when it celebrated its centenary. It all looked so *small*. The forbidding Headmaster's room seemed insignificant and the pond at Whepstead Hall, opposite, seemed quite tiny. In the far-off days of which I write it all seemed so big and vast.

My grandparents on my father's side were also farming people, and had retired to 'New House', now called 'The

Butler's Hall, Hawstead, birth place of the author.

Beeches', just a short walk from Butler's Hall. On grandpa's death I was given his watch, complete with solid gold chain. I shall pass this on to my grandson Russell.

Grandma lived on to be ninety-five; a remarkable old lady and rather a martinet. Aunt Ada kept house for her and played the organ at Hawstead Church for forty-one years without a break! When no longer able to attend Church, grandma would follow the prayer-book service at the same time it was being held at Hawstead Church.

We were taken to Hawstead Church regularly by our parents and we loved going. So much rubbish is written these days about 'forcing' youngsters to attend Church.

The Rector of Hawstead, Leslie Mercer, held the benefice for forty-four years. He did not wear a dog collar, but instead wore a winged collar with a white tie, plus a tall, silk hat which gave way to a trilby in later years.

Hawstead Church is singularly beautiful and historic. It is literally filled with monuments and stained glass. There are horse-box pews and an original 'sanctus bell' on the Rood screen. There are two Norman doorways and inside, under a richly ornamented arch, lies the stone effigy of Eustace — Fitz Eustace, who may have been christened at the ancient font when it was new. Here he has rested in his armour, legs crossed and a dog at his feet, since the last crusade was nearing its close in 1270. Many of the other memorials, including a funeral-helmet, are in memory of the Drury family — great benefactors to the Parish.

They entertained Good Queen Bess at their moated mansion, Hawstead Place, in 1578 and their family associations gave their name to a famous London Theatre district — Drury Lane. It was Sir William Drury who had the honour of receiving the Virgin Queen and tradition has it that she dropped her silver handled fan into the moat at Hawstead Place.

When Cullum wrote his history of Hawstead, in the eighteenth century, he mentioned a giant figure of Hercules holding a club in one hand and "discharging a perennial stream of water by the urinary passage, into a curved, stone basin". This statue was stolen some years ago but, in 1978, Mr. Powell, the present owner and occupier, recovered it and restored it, including this unusual "fountain". It was unveiled at celebrations marking the four-hundred year anniversary of the visit of Queen Bess.

Sir William Drury died in a duel in France and his son Robert inherited the estate. The latter was knighted in the seige of Rohan, in 1591, when he was only fifteen years of age. He is best remembered as the Patron of Dr. John Donne, whose very first printed poem was the famous elegy, "1611", on Drury's daughter. It contains these remarkable lines:

All Saints Church, Hawstead. This interior view was taken in 1932.

"Her pure and eloquent blood spoke in her cheeks, and so distinctly wrought that one might almost say her body thought".

A more pathetic memorial inscription in the Church always impressed me as a lad and still does so. It commemorates a young Drury who died in extreme infancy. "Shee little promised much . . . too soon untyed. Shee only dreamt shee lived . . . and then shee dyed".

I have already mentioned the Rector Leslie Mercer. I think he must have liked me for, in later years, he would sometimes ask me to dinner. He kept a housekeeper and a Butler-Valet who waited at table. He never forgot my brother Maurice's first visit to a Church service. Maurice had been warned not to talk, and indeed, behaved splendidly. On coming out, he commented: "That naughty man (meaning the Rector) kept on talking all the time".

The Rector's ancient car, a 1908 Hotchkiss with high wheels, was well-known in the district. It had a mass of brass, acetyline lighting. I was given the generator years later and used it to provide gas for my magic-lantern. The car had a high back and the hood did not cover poor old Sidney Kerridge, the driver. The hooter was a whistle embodied in the exhaust pipe. The Rector's sudden passing in 1929 was a shock to the parish and I certainly lost a very good friend.

My sister and I used to go to aunt for music lessons. My completely non-mathematical mind could not take it, but Molly persevered and plays well. In later years, however, I learned to play tolerably well by ear and could harmonize. I have been known to play the Church organ and have always enjoyed singing lustily.

In my boyhood there were of course no refrigerators. Big country houses would have an ice-pit partly underground where ice could be stored for a limited period only. Pigs were killed "into the house", which meant that cottager and farmer alike would periodically kill a pig, sometimes communally. Many of the joints would be salted in salting pots, big earthenware pots, which now fetch good prices in antique shops. Other joints would be smoked and cured for bacon. There was no wastage at all. Lights and liver made 'fry' and some intestines were washed and cooked. The small intestines were used in sausage making and the odd pieces went into brawn or pork-cheese as it was sometimes called, and even the bladder became Philip's first-ever football. I wonder how many of today's professionals have ever seen a pig's bladder, let alone kicked one for a ball?

One of my other very early recollections from Butler's Hall was the day on which one of the carthorses died from a twisted gut. Ben Talbot's knacker's cart came to fetch it away and my father pushed me indoors, but I watched the sad scene from a window.

The cart was drawn alongside and ropes were attached to the corpse. The windlass affixed to the cart was just like the one above our well to which I have already referred. The fallen giant was gradually hauled on to the cart and covered in part by a filthy cloth. Drawn by the knacker's own pony, this animal-hearse moved forward into the sunshine of an unseeing world. At the front, Dobbin's grotesque head hung down and sticking out at the back a hoof dangled stiffly. I still get a feeling of depression when, at an auction, I see good horses sold to be put down for the value of their meat, because in this car mad age nobody tries to keep and use them.

Periodically an itinerant harness-maker nicknamed "Norker" Hudgell from Lawshall would come and spend a couple of days on the farm repairing the carthorse and pony harnesses. He would invariably complain of the lack of oiling with neatsfoot oil. The neglected harness would handle hard and lack 'life' when he came to mend and make do!

In the summer of 1914 we had the second of two holidays at Southend-on-Sea and were there when war broke out. Mother took us — Dad never left the farm — and we stayed with an aunt who kept house for old John Stevens. He was a dear old man who rode a tricycle and still played cricket when over ninety. He taught us to play Bagatelle and to be reverent at family prayers.

When Southend was bombed they came to live at Mill House, Hartest and when staying there with them I entered my first working windmill. I shall not forget the thrill; every board and every strut seemed to vibrate and come to life as those giant sails kept turning. Later on, I sketched and photographed over 150 of these remarkable structures — many of which are no longer extant.

Chapter 2

In that most fateful year, 1914, Butler's Hall was sold by auction and, my father being out-bid, we had to move to the much smaller Bryers Farm, Hawstead. This was already being farmed by him but he felt the move very much as he had brought Butler's Hall round from dereliction. Smaller than Butler's Hall, the house at Bryers Farm had a steeply pitched thatched roof. Bryers Farm was historic, being built in the 16th century. The farm was mostly reclaimed woodland and in September 1611, Sir Robert Drury bestowed it upon a faithful servant, Gabriel Catchpole, for "service already done and performed and hereafter to be performed". The bequest was to last forty years and the rent was "one peppercorn" to be paid every Michaelmas.

We also farmed "Lamp Land" a small field, the rent from which was originally bequeathed towards keeping a lamp burning continually before the altar in the church at Hawstead. Within sight of Bryers Farm was 'Jacobs Well', said to have magic properties in that the driest of summers failed to exhaust its supply. It was an open pool surrounded by oak fencing and a stone bore the inscription: 'Empty me — empty the sea'. The old name for the road was 'Caldwell Strete'. In 1935, when Council houses were built nearby, the well was enclosed and a pump erected above it. In the drought of 1921 this old well supplied water for householders and livestock all over the parish, but if emptied at night it always filled by the morning. I am so glad that a couple of years ago my niece, Angela, and her husband, Terry,

'Jacobs Well', Hawstead's magic well.

named their new house next to Bryers Farm, 'Caldwell', and thus have preserved the old name.

Our method of transport apart from cycles was horse and trap. 'Venus' was an unusually light coloured roan mare with a starred forehead and the same age as myself. An iron-tyred cart served for carting farm stuff, including trips to the Mill, but for market days and Sundays we used the 'best' cart, a rubber tyred varnished trap. We youngsters sat on a box in front. Everybody 'sat forward' when going uphill and reversed the arrangement at each decline of the road. We drove to Church, stabling being provided there. Soldiers stationed at Hardwick Park gave an added excitement when they attended Church Parade there. On Friday, we Hawstead School children attended Church and although we found the Litany dull, we loved the Rector's simple talks. I recall so well that he used the early experiments in wireless (then taking place) to illustrate the unseen workings of the Holy Spirit.

The village school was a one room affair, even smaller than the one at Whepstead. The urinals and little privies were outside and an iron pump over a well, provided the water. A tortoise stove provided the warmth. Slates and slate pencils were used in the infants section and a monitor would go outside to sharpen the pencils on a brick wall!

I recall reciting a poem which began: 'Two little kittens had lost their mittens . . .' at a school concert in 1915. Toys consisted of a bowling-hoop made of wood for the girls, but a blacksmith made an iron hoop for the boys. Spinning tops were the rage for a few weeks, then it would be pop-guns. The latter were made from a length of alder wood from which the pith had been removed by a red-hot poker. A hazel ram-rod would be shaped by a pocket-knife. Beans were often used as ammunition but a compound bullet of wet paper was better! The longer the gun the louder the pop. A whistle was made from an ash or sycamore branch cut from the hedge and incisions made in the bark. A hollowed piece of alder

Hawstead village school, taken in 1929.

was opened in the middle in which was bent a steel spring from mother's stays. This made a most effective pea-shooter! A length of hazel, bent and made taut with string, made a bow and a reed tipped by a piece of alder and notched at the other end was all that was needed for a bow and arrow outfit.

In the playground the girls often played separately from the boys. The former played 'Kiss in the ring', 'Here comes a lad riding by', 'Poor Mary sits a-weeping', 'Here we come gathering nuts and may' and 'Oranges and lemons'. As they skipped, they would count thus: 'silk, satin, cotton, rags' over and over again; or 'salt, mustard, vinegar, pepper'; or again, 'tinker, tailor, soldier, sailor, rich man, poor man, beggar man, thief'; 'London bridge is broken down — my fair ladye'.

Boys would often join in the above but we had our own tough games. One of these was 'Sheep, sheep, come home' called by a boy at the end of the playground. Our reply was 'We're afraid'. 'Afraid of what?'. 'The Wolf''. Then he would say, 'The Wolf is gone to Devonshire and won't be home for seven year'. At this we made a concerted dash to the end, during which he waylaid whom he could, and those would then become 'wolves' with him until every 'sheep' had been caught.

There was also 'Bumble Alley'. A big boy stood facing the playground wall as an anchor. Four others bent their backs and clung to each other and to him. The rest would make a running jump as far as possible on to the backs of others. Soon everybody fell, shouting the words, 'Bumble Alley, Bumble Alley. One, two, three, all off!'

On Empire Day the Chairman of the School Managers would unfurl and hoist a Union Jack and we were taught to salute it and to respect it. My word! What a change from those days and in many respects a change for the worse.

On St. Valentine's Day we would be marched to the Rectory drive and would sing a ditty which none of us really understood. I give it from memory:

'Good morning, Valentine. Good morning Valentine,
Plait your hair as I do mine,
Two in front and two behind.
Good morning Valentine. Good morning Valentine.'

Many farmer's horses in the 1914-18 war were commandeered for military service and they had to get cars. 'Venus' our cob however, was too light in colour, so we kept her. A favourite Sunday evening drive was to Chadacre Hall, a mansion belonging to the Weller-Poley family. Here, Uncle John Honeywood (my mother's brother) lived for the duration to manage the estate and look after the place. We loved it, but little did I dream that in less than eight years it would become an agricultural college and that I should be one of its first students.

The author's parents on a day trip to Felixstowe.

Mother baked our own bread in those days at Bryers Farm and it was my job, every Saturday morning, to cut up the faggots with which mother 'fired' the brick-oven. A special evening treat would be Apple Turnover, after which I would go down to the Green and waylay Daniel Alcock, the postman (later Callard), who would bring Lloyds Weekly News. There were of course no Sunday papers.

Illustrated papers and magazines were called 'Gays' and an early photographer was called 'a likeness taker'. Papers in some parishes were provided by the Squire and Parson who would place them in a village Reading Room. Both at Littlebury and Roxwell, where I served as Vicar, there was still a Reading Room in 1979.

A bout of pneumonia at the age of seven left me with lung weakness for the rest of my life. Once again Dr. Hinnell came out and this time his pony-trap had given place to a car. From that day until I was sixteen I did not see a doctor professionally but have had my share of medical help since. We treated sprains and strains with 'Hoss oils' which was another name for the famous Elliman's Embrocation, but we always had their strong mixture, specially for horses and cattle.

The war had raised the value of mole-skins to nine pence and this was a fortune to me. Dad caught them I skinned them and nailed them to a board. Subsequently, we took them to a dealer who, most appropriately, had his stinking headquarters in Skinner Street, Bury St. Edmunds at the rear of Cupola House which is now an ancient hostelry and was once the home of Daniel Defoe, author of Robinson Crusoe.

Hawstead was not without its links with literature, for Joseph Hall, one time Rector, was the Jacobean Divine who later became Bishop of Norwich. A recorded local utterance of Bishop Hall suggests that, even in those far off days, medieval ladies liked a spot of paint and powder. One day he cried out from Hawstead's fine pulpit, 'Ye plaster-faced Jezebels. One day God will wipe your faces with fire and brimstone".

The other literary figure was Sir John Cullum, one of the Cullums from nearby Hardwick Mansion. He was historian of the parish and was Rector of Hawstead in the eighteenth century. Cullum gave the world a parish history before Gilbert White gave us Selborne. Cullum compiled a list of wild flowers peculiar to the district and also a valuable dictionary of local dialect. Both Hall and Cullum are commemorated in stained glass in the Church, as is John Powell, an ancestor of Baden-Powell. They lived at Hammond's Farm, now farmed by my brother. When I was a lad a beautiful timbered barn was demolished there and taken down to Clacton-on-Sea and re-erected as Tudor House. The old Malting House at Hawstead, opposite Jacobs Well, was demolished in 1929, and shipped to America for re-erection. Alfred Blundell lived at the old Hall for a time and there painted pictures, some of which were eventually hung in the Royal Academy.

Daphne Hammonde was a poetess who lived in Hawstead all her life and Edmund Blunden lived for a time at Hawstead Place. He was a popular member of our village cricket team.

Blunden had served in the war and his subsequent 'war' book *'The Undertones of War'* was very well received. I regard him, however, as pre-eminently the poet of the countryside who was unrivalled as an interpreter of English rural life. *'The Waggoner'*, 1920 and *'The Shepherd'*, 1922 spring to mind. But I like best his *'Almswomen'* inspired by the residents of Hawstead Almshouses (who used to attend Church and sit together wearing their special uniform black bonnets) and his *'Forefathers'*.

Returning home after a spell as Professor of English at Tokyo University, he wrote a poem entitled, *'Return'*. His emotions many must have shared.

> *"How stands that man enchanted,*
> *Who after seas and mountains crossed,*
> *Finds his old threshold so long scanted*
> *With not a rose, nor robin, lost."*

I kept in touch with him by correspondence and when I was at the Theological College in 1936 he wrote to me: "Let your religious and literary life be united. You have admirable advantages and an experience of life as good as Oxford, or even Cambridge, caps and gowns!". He died at Long Melford early in 1974. He looked at some of my writings and subsequently reviewed a little book of mine in 'Times Literary Supplement'. But I am anticipating and want to keep this effort chronological, as far as I can.

I was taken to see the Peace Celebrations in Bury St. Edmunds in 1918 and watched the torchlight procession from Angel Hill, wondering just how many similar scenes the old Abbey Gate had witnessed. Bury was our market town and we loved going there. Dad was a well-known figure at the Market with his buttonhole in its water-filled holder, and in this respect I have followed in his steps ever since.

Once we gave a cat to some friends in Bury. It was taken there in a covered basket. Some days later a bedraggled much travelled puss was back home again. Can anybody explain this remarkable instinct? The same pair of blue-tits, for many years, nested in the tool box of a derelict binder in Bryers Orchard; and two Jackdaws, which we reared from the nest, would perch on our shoulders as we walked round the farm and parish and would always return to perch at the house every nightfall. A Suffolk horse sold at an Uncle's farm sale went 15 miles to its new owner beyond Long Melford. A week later he appeared at his old stables in Hartest in the early hours, having broken out of the yard of his new home. This homing instinct has never been explained.

We too were "home-birds". We did not travel far; country folk didn't in those days and were content. Apart from school holidays at Hartest and a couple at Brixton, I recall visits to Little Maplestead, Essex, where Dad's youngest brother, Wilfred, had established a fine herd of prize-winning Red Roll cattle. Four of these were later killed by lightning in 1929. With cars still not commonly used in our circle, a great treat was an occasional day-trip to Felixstowe or Yarmouth with the Garrard family in one of their butcher's vans. These were bad times for Mother — a life-long sufferer from travel sickness and latterly she could not attempt such journeys at all.

Bryers Wood was a great joy although only five acres in extent. It was relaxing to just sit on a fallen branch and enjoy the stillness, only to discover a seething mass of living movement all around. The birds and animals plus insects, would assert themselves in this small wilderness. Spring brought a carpeting of oxlips and anemones to be followed by bluebells and daffodils. I had planted the daffodils around the wood. Our horsekeeper, Charlie Long, had grafted garden roses on to the wild briers and left them to flourish in their wild state. The effect was lovely. Two unusual wild flowers grew there in the orchard — the Bee Orchis and the Fritillary (snake's headed lily). I recall dragging my young brother, the dog and two kittens up to the wood, and standing in my shirt, conducted an open-air service with them as the congregation.

We had a white house cow called 'Sleepy', which allowed us to ride anywhere on her back. Occasionally she would throw up her heels and gallop under an apple tree in the five acre orchard, when the luckless rider would fall heavily. We took a similar risk with 'Billy', the Ram (or Tup as we called them), who served our little flock of Southdown sheep. We had many a butting duel with him by getting on all fours and encouraging him to charge us. I once brought up a motherless litter of pigs on the bottle. It was easier to do this with motherless lambs, who would follow us anywhere on the farm and indoors if we let them. We also had many pet rabbits.

In 1920 my sister and I began attending the West Suffolk County Secondary School, which meant cycling five miles into Bury each day and back at night. In those days flinty roads gave us great experience in roadside puncture-mending. Many children had double that journey, contrasting with the short-distance school buses of the present day.

Schooldays were certainly *not* my happiest. I was a dud at Mathematics but I liked English, History and Poetry. My shortness of breath meant that I did not excel at sports although I was keen enough. A retrospective outlook and an inferiority complex made me sensitive and cowardly. I made very few real friends, but some of them did cycle out on Saturdays to sample the delights of a farm, together with Mother's excellent cooking. My school reports were not good and if ever I got into trouble at school it meant more trouble at home. The present day tendency, however, seems to be that if a teacher so much as reprimands or punishes a youngster, he or she is faced by an irate parent next morning. We have listened too long to the 'do gooders' in sparing the rod and the result has been utterly harmful to the youngsters.

What a terrible situation these days when some teachers are, by example, showing children how to go slow and strike and mount picket lines!

Those Christmases at Bryers Farm are worth a mention. They were happy days with little money to spare for frivolities. We were thrilled with the few things which came our way via caring parents. We walked to Church and on our return would meet up with postman Callard doing his tiring round by cycle or on foot. At lunch we were joined by Aunt Ada the organist. A day or two previously I had been sent round the village with gifts of rabbits from my father to the occupants of the Metcalf and the Drury Almshouses. The former came to Church wearing special black bonnets. We were also joined at lunch by Dad's bachelor brother, Thomas Wright, of Ixworth, who would drive the dozen miles in a smart trap with a cream coloured pony. This turnout he used regularly in his rounds as 'Relieving Officer' for the poor — a position he combined with that of School Attendance Officer and Registrar for a wide area.

In his capacity as 'Relieving Officer' he and his pony-trap were sometimes pressed into service for a very sad errand, conveying a mentally deranged person to Bury Station en route for Melton Asylum, near Woodbridge. The patient sat in the little pony trap handcuffed to the village policeman with my uncle driving the pony.

On Christmas day faithful Charlie Long would have been to bait the carthorses, Depper, Snip and Blossom, together with Venus the pony, giving them that extra bit of corn for Christmas dinner. Down the road, Percy Mason would be faithfully tending the sheep at Fyletts Farm. After tea we would gather round the piano and Aunt Ada would accompany our carol singing.

When the time came, Uncle's pony would be harnessed for the return journey to Ixworth and Philip would be given a shilling for tying a bunch of straw or hay and filling a bag of chaff for the pony. A white Christmas was somewhat rare although I recall going out on the roads to cut pathways for man and beast through the deep snow drifts. Mud, fog and rain were more common.

On Christmas Eve I would drag a 'mud-hoe' to tidy the yard and give extra straw bedding to the cattle and pigs. This was a long time ago but in the year 1963 I went down to the Grotto of that rather gaudy Church of the Nativity, in Bethlehem and knelt on the very spot of our Lord's birth. Afterwards we were shown outside to a typical Palestinian Stable or cow byre — not nearly the cosy comfortable place beloved of the designers of Christmas cards. His birthplace would have been fouled by dung and dirt; perhaps infested by insects. No cosy cottage; no maternity ward; nothing even approaching the cow-parlour or stables of a modern farm.

I shall never know quite how much I owe to my mother's prayers, teaching and shining example. The great privilege of regular attendance at Church taught me so much and gave me a knowledge of The Psalter, the Old Prayer Book and Hymns Ancient and Modern, which have been such a stand-by.

I think that children need to be introduced to Christian teaching first by the New Testament approach. You see, childhood and adolescence are the times for hero worship and Christ is the hero whom mothers, teachers and Ministers should be showing forth. The great Adventurer, challenging conventions, confronting his enemies without fear, facing hardship, disappointment and death, the cross and passion, then becomes a reality. Youngsters have an inborn awe of the loveliness of God's world and if they are taught to associate all goodness with God the Father, they will be at least on the right road and will more readily learn to discern right from wrong.

my Uncle lived there. I had left school in 1922 and in October of that year I had become a Chadacre student. I discovered that the stable loft had become a dormitory and the open courtyard had been covered in to become a dining hall with balcony. Male students entered in October and left in March to work on farms until the 'second year' course began in the following October. In the summer, girl students were welcomed for training in dairying, poultry-keeping and horticulture. Boy students took part in the practical farm work and were divided into classes.

On 'Milking-week', the porter called us at 5.30 a.m. and the road down to the Home Farm cowshed was completely mud-bound. Rubber Wellingtons were unknown and we wore breeches with boots and buskins which we scrubbed daily. The cows there were a mixed Shorthorn herd and were later replaced by Red Polls. On those icy mornings we would sing "Nothing could be sweeter than to milk the heifer Greta in the morning" and other ribald songs. Alternating with Milking-week was horse-feeding when we groomed and fed the magnificent Suffolk horses either at Home Farm or Rivetts, the latter again being very familiar ground.

After hand milking we would start the milk separator and the steam boiler whilst others mucked out the cows and did a round of the poultry runs with food, water and egg-basket. We returned to the Institute for 8 a.m. breakfast and from 9 a.m. till midday we were in the lecture-room or laboratory. At 2 p.m. we reported for farm classes. These included land measuring, carpentry, blacksmith's work, gardening, harness-mending and potato picking. There was also butter and cheese-making, hedge laying, hurdle making and threshing with steam tackle. After tea there was football or boxing, an hour's prep, a 9 o'clock roll call and bed and lights out at 9.30 p.m. Under Principal John Robinson, discipline was very rigid and instead of corporal punishment we would be given an extra week's milking.

Only two students had a motor-bike. I think of this when I pass the Writtle College car park in 1980 and note the huge array of student's cars. So greatly have things changed farm-wise that I have been able to use certain lecture notes made at Chadacre for my four books on old time farming-methods.

Hedging class at Chadacre College.

When I was a Chadacre student the livestock consisted of 120 head of cattle (30 milkers), 14 Suffolk Horses, a few sheep, 150 pigs and flocks of Rhode Island Red hens, plus those of the white Wyandotte and white Leghorn breeds.

Mechanization was almost unknown except for barn machinery for root cutting, milling and cattle-cake crushing. This range of machinery was powered by an oil-engine started with a blow lamp. Each year at the Suffolk Show, Chadacre students formed the main competitors at the working dairy. We made study visits to Ransomes of Ipswich (still building traction engines and threshing drums) and to Fisons Manure works at Bramford.

On Sundays we marched down to Hartest Church and, as might be expected with an adolescent community, we could become boorish and uncouth. It was not the fault of Henry Wisdom, the Rector of Hartest, who took a lively evangelical interest in our souls. He had spent some time in the Australian bush. He was a good horseman and by his riding and driving he visited his parish and us, his outlying parishioners. How little did I then dream that, in 1978, I would be an old parson riding and driving my cob, "Topper', in the same manner.

On Speech day, March 1924, I netted a couple of prizes and also received the Institute diploma at the hands of Vicountess Elveden, later to become Lady Iveagh. I still have the diploma and value it greatly, even though it bears the date 1924.

In April 1923 I was confirmed at Hawstead Church by the Bishop of St. Edmundsbury & Ipswich, Dr. Augustus David who soon became Bishop of Liverpool and one day, some 16 years later, was to Ordain me to the sacred Ministry.

After Chadacre I returned home to live and work at Bryers Farm. When quite a small boy I was initiated into the mysteries of birth and death, by getting up at night to hold the lantern for my father when a cow was calving, a ewe lambing or a horse ill. I had likewise learned about sex in a natural unembarrassing way from animals, beginning in the earlier years when I kept rabbits. I was a good, dry-handed milker and liked looking after pigs and poultry and seeing to our small flock of Southdown sheep.

Staff and students of the Chadacre Institute, 1924.

So much romance has been woven around seedtime, haysel and harvest but to me these seasons meant times when tempers were quick, nerves were strained and always there was this everlasting fight with the weather. I remember once we were drilling barley and a chap helping us seemed slow with filling up the drill. "Yeow wait a minnit", replied George. "Moi mother waited nine months for me". Quick came the retort from my father, "And a pretty beggar she got, too". And they say country folk are dull-witted.

I so often find myself quoting my father's sayings. If I had made a faulty purchase he would say, "Bought wit is best if you don't buy too dearly". "The earth is a mother to all weeds but only a foster-mother to corn." "Never harrow a wheat field during an east wind." "A man who don't love a horse isn't capable of loving a woman." He would coin the advice given on baby care to make it apply to the good husbandry needed on heavy soil. "Treat it like a baby. Keep its face clean and its bottom dry", i.e. keep the weeds down and drain the land well. Of an unthrifty wife he would remark, "Her old man gave her a nest-egg bank account but she wouldn't lay to it". "Where there's no sense there's no feeling." To myself, to silence me he would say "Shut up. You'd talk the hind leg off a donkey". Of a short sermon he would say, "T'was like a donkey's gallop — soon over". To a visitor wearing a nice hat he would remark, "If that ow'd hat ever have pups, save one for me". "A whistling woman and a crowing hen is neither use to God nor man."

My Uncle Thomas once gave me a pen-knife but insisted that I paid a penny for it. To accept a gift knife was said to be unlucky. If a thunderstorm occurred at mealtimes, knives would be put away for fear of attracting lightning. To sleep in direct moonlight was said to cause lunacy, or at least nightmares. At a household where bees were kept and a death occurred, somebody would go to the hives and solemnly "tell the bees". Failure to do so would (so they said) lead to another death in the family within the year or to the death of the bees.

During a drought my father would say, "A pity fine weather ever did any harm", and when speaking of a person to whom favour had been shown he would say, "Oh he (or she) is one of the white hen's chickens".

My father loved his gun and was an excellent shot. On the other hand he was not at all keen on my village "cricketing" and "footballing" activities because they tempted me away from the farm on Saturday afternoons. My brother Maurice could beat me at both games. I was secretary to both football and cricket clubs and the field of play was the large village green (thirty-five acres) at Hawstead.

Only a narrow strip was mown for the cricket pitch and the outfield was rough grass partially grazed by Marsh's flock of Suffolk sheep. We had no boundaries whatsoever and ran six runs for a lost ball, so that thirty to forty runs was a good score. We cycled to matches with bats and pads strapped on to our bikes.

Maurice, on leaving school, was apprenticed to the Bury ironworks of Robert Boby where, among other things, he learned to sing, "The Red Flag", much to my father's disapproval. I, myself, put in several months at Byham Hall, Great Maplestead, Essex where I fed the sows, milked seven cows, churned and made the butter, went hoeing in the fields and washed-up after the paying guests had fed. I received half a crown a week, paid monthly. This was in 1926.

The following year I won a prize at a furrow drawing match at Stanningfield using a pair of horses on a wooden framed plough. That year I spent several months at a local Ford depot in Bury picking up a little knowledge of tractors and cars.

In 1928 I had an appendix operation at Bury Hospital and learned to admire the members of the nursing profession.

About this time I began reporting local news for local papers, being paid a halfpenny a line, and soon was writing verse and articles illustrated by my own photographs and sketches.

Rejection-slips poured in at first but later years saw acceptance from quite respectable newspapers and periodicals. The subjects included; old houses, farming, local and rural history, plus windmills, to sketch or photograph for which I would cycle many miles.

In November 1929, three weeks before Christmas, Bryers farmhouse was partially destroyed by fire due to a defective

The original Bryers Farm . . . before the fire of 1929.

. . after its partial destruction by fire in 1929.

. . and as it is today.

chimney which included a smouldering oak beam in its structure. I dashed into Bury St. Edmunds on my Douglas motorcycle and led the fire-engine back to our home. There was not a telephone in the parish at that time. Neighbours were splendid. Whilst Dad was getting out the best bits of parlour furniture and Mother was rescuing bedding and the like, I made a bee-line for irreplacable stuff including certificates belonging to my sister who after qualifying at Norwich Teachers Training College had begun a teaching career in Birmingham. Our staircases were spiral and one had been removed when we moved in 1914 to facilitate getting big stuff upstairs. Now, with the roof blazing, there was no time for such a procedure.

We shared 'New House' with Aunt Ada during the re-building and our terrier, 'Togo', could not be persuaded to leave the house. That Christmas we had a hundred fine turkeys to be protected. Subsequently, I became so interested in fire-fighting that in World War II, when curate at Saffron Walden, I became a part-time fireman.

Not long after our fire, the telephone was installed in the village Post Office where Mrs. Brewster, the post mistress, for a very meagre sum brought up a family and conducted the Post Office business in one room. I felt a brute going there at meal times but never do I recall her being other than cheerfully obliging.

There are thirty-five acres of Hawstead Green and it was with mixed feelings that I saw it broken up in 1942 under stress of war. Here indeed history was made, Common rights usurped, and virgin soil broken. It had seen football and cricket being played for long years and it was much used for grazing. Subsequently it was re-grassed and became a Green again.

What a lot I have learned from these 'sons of the soil' and rural craftsmen. One such was Charlie Long, our faithful and versatile horse-keeper, who had a big family in the days when money was almost non-existent. He could do all the horse drawn tillage jobs and stack and thatch. This dear man who had so few of life's pleasantries possessed a wonderful sense of humour and even the vilest and most unpleasant situations which could occur on the farm calendar would be met with a joke from Charlie. His sayings were also very

Brother Maurice driving our first tractor watched by Dad. These implements were formerly horse-drawn.

Another Haysel scene at Bryers Farm. Jack Hanslip with the scythe and Charlie Long sitting on the horse drawn mower.

This old Hornsby binder was completing its 27th harvest!

The last load, which the author himself loaded on to a 100-year-old wagon then clambered down and took the photograph.

Carting sheaves in 1929 at Bryers Farm, Hawstead.

much to the point. If he wanted to describe an utterly mean person he would say, "He won't see anybody in want — he'll shut his eyes". Or again, "He's so mean he'd lick a farden (farthing) out of a turd.", or "He's so mean he'd rob a child of its breakfast.".

I had been "thatcher's boy" for "Banty" Hale as part of my Chadacre tuition and used to do it for Charlie Long. Nowadays, we old-timers miss the rows of stacks which graced the farms after harvesting. At Bryers we also had two sets of iron "staddles" which enabled two round stacks to be built raised a few feet from the ground. The others were rectangular gable-ended stacks or sometimes boat shaped with rounded ends.

After harvest we would pick out the best, cleanest wheat-straw which I would scatter into sizeable heaps and then dampen it with buckets of water and a flick of the wrist.

I would then draw it into big "sheaves" called "yellums". Five or six small bundles made up a yellum. A crotched hazel stick with an attached line was used to carry the yellum up the big thatching ladder whenever Charlie called. He would lay out the yellum, and braid it in with hazel broatches and tarred-cord. The combing down and shearing of the eaves came later. So well were the stacks built that it was a great reproach to have to 'shore' one stack up with timber to prevent it falling. Today the only stacks we see are heaps of straw-bales or hay; so greatly and thoroughly has the combine-harvester taken over.

I have mentioned broatches. These were split hazel rods for thatching. Each year a small portion "slop" of Bryers Wood was cut down by either Charles Elsden or Jim Smith, both expert woodmen. They would sit in a roughly made shelter and with the simplest of tools, fashion broatches and, with the Ash saplings would make hurdles. The hurdles were used for folding sheep on turnips and kale and there isn't a handier fencing asset on a farm where a hedge gap needs first aid, or when refractory animals need guidance to prevent a breakaway. I have used them with success for sheep, cattle, pigs and donkeys.

Once however, a sizeable pig escaped my hurdle and ran headlong into a horse-pond. I was full of foreboding but the pig (who had never before left the stye) proceeded to swim to the other side of the pond with strong strokes. So wonderfully has nature provided for their safety that they are inherent swimmers and so, also, are rabbits!

Another old-timer who worked for us was Harry Gooch of Lawshall. He had never left Suffolk but had curiously enough developed a most refined manner of speech. He referred to everybody, rich or poor, as 'neighbour', and this is interesting because that, precisely, is the definition of the "Old bor" prefix of Suffolk dialect. It is purely and simply a shortening of the word "neighbour". Every Christmas Harry and his wife did an itinerary of farms in the area to kill, pluck and roughly dress the turkeys, and it was he who taught me to pluck and truss poultry — a job I have frequently done since.

All of them loved a drop of my father's home brewed beer, and this they were never denied. Brewing days centred around seed time, harvest, haymaking and sugar beeting. Brewing days were busy days for me. I had the job of pumping and carrying the large quantities of water needed. Here is my father's recipe:

2 bushels of Malt

1 stone of sugar

3lbs. of hops
Three penny worth of yeast
50 gallons of water
(a pinch of black malt adds colour to the beer)

Put the water (after boiling it in the copper) into the mash-tub, 7 pails-full of boiling water to 3 pails-full of cold water. Shoot the malt onto the water and stir carefully. Then fill up the tub with water. Leave for four hours and then draw off the liquid "sweet wert". Put this back into the copper and boil for four hours. Strain this into the second mash-tub and when the beer is luke-warm, yeast may be added. This process is called "setting the beer to work". It can now be left to cool, after which it is skimmed and "turned" into the barrel. A "second wert" may be brewed by adding water to the grains after the first brew has been drawn off.

Nothing was wasted. The horses and cattle relished the grains, and the spent hops were a grand fertilizer!

Nobody would teach me to drive a car so I was determined to buy one and teach myself. A foolish decision for some-body of my financial standing, but youth had its fling. At the time I had been working to fulfil a road contract for my father. Following an application of flint and sand in 1927, granite was being steam rollered on to the Lawshall, Bury Road. My job was to 'horse' the watercart with 'Snip', the faithful strawberry-roan mare, and keep the surface wet for the roller and brooms. This has long since been superseded by the Tarmac process. Working with a broom was a workman who sold me a Humberette for £5. She was of pre-1914 vintage; a small car with a twin air-cooled engine, a dummy radiator and a long push rod with which to tickle the car-burettor for easy starting. I found out afterwards that Bert, the previous owner, had pushed her more miles than he had driven her. I had the same experience and within one week the connecting rod had broken into one of the cylinders and the car was ruined. This model had long since been obsolete, spares were unobtainable and I sold her for £1 for scrap. What would she be worth in today's values when anything ancient is cherished beyond our wildest dreams and restored?

In a former chapter I recall my early addiction to wind-mills. At Hawstead I lived within sight of a fine post-mill

this story sometimes to critics who have condemned me for being a 'Hunting Parson'.

We have mentioned pheasants, but what has happened to the humble partridge? Until I was twenty, the keepers on the large estates would "bush" the stubble after the harvest rakings had been carted. "Bushing" meant sticking short hedgerow branches at irregular intervals over the stubble. This was a deterrent against night-poachers with drag-nets which they used to enmesh the partridges as they clustered in coveys for bed-time. Partridges do not perch high as do pheasants. Modern poison sprays have accounted for the huge losses among the youngsters of these wonderful little game birds.

Work was hard on the farms in 1920s and early thirties with no mechanization to ease the work load. Now at seventy-two, and in not too good health, folk wonder that I don't walk for fun. Like many a farmer's boy I walked a huge mileage in those days following ploughs, harrow drills and like implements. Such mileage was never measured nor appreciated and that, dear reader, may be why I don't go for ten-mile walks before breakfast these days.

Another tiring job was "grassing", i.e. digging out by fork, pails-full of spear-grass or twitch and burning it on the headland. Hedge-cutting and scything also tested the muscles; hay-making and threshing were even worse. Muck-filling from an open shed, where bullocks had wintered and trodden in the muck and litter, was a cruel job, often done by a tractor-scoop today. We always cut around a harvest field before we dreamed of bringing in the binder. It was hard work scything and tying-up behind. Today the combine-harvester is driven straight into the field. Spoilation and wastage is ignored in the mad rush to "get the job finished" and where husbandry is a by-word.

Market days and Agricultural Shows were the typical day outings but thanks to my sister (by this time teaching in Colchester) I once had a day-trip to Belgium. Leaving Harwich at 11 p.m. we made Zebrugge at dawn and spent a long day sight-seeing in Heyst and Bruges before embarking that same night at 11 p.m.

The cereal, vegetable and fruit varieties of that day are seldom heard of today. Wheats then included Benefactor,

Little Joss, Squarehead Master and Chevallier barley. Potatoes were Sharp's Express, Arran Comrade and International kidney — the latter being a show variety. The old trees in Bryers orchard, Blenheim-orange, Sopsy Wine, Ribstone Pippins and Codlins, were varieties of apples.

Much more care is taken these days over cereal seed-corn. In the old days people grew their own seed then, after a year or two, would exchange seed with a neighbour so that the variety stock didn't become soil-sick. I remember James Savage of New Hall Farm, Stanningfield telling my father he was exchanging seed-wheat with a farmer in the Fens, at a place called "Black Bank". Thomas Tusser knew this practise and in his famous "Husbandry", for August he says:

"Once harvest dispatched get wench's and boys
And into the barn before all other tois.
Choice seed to be picked and trimly well fyd (dressed)
For seed may no longer from threshing abide.

Get seed aforehand in a readiness had,
Or better provide if thine own be too bad.
Be careful of seed, or else such as ye sow,
Be suer at harvest to reap or to mow."

The late 1920s saw a real farming slump but the introduction of sugar beet gave promise of a guaranteed price for something. It was hard, unpleasant work especially in bad weather on our heavy land. Today it is all mechanised. When the price dropped, our accounts showed no better except that by extra manuring and soil preparation the following corn-crop would benefit. It seemed to me that the factory got the sugar but we were getting "beat". It says much for the British farmer that in subsequent years we produced our own sugar in this island. Corn prices were halved — I saw farmers hawking their corn samples from merchant to merchant without getting a bid — this was on Bury Corn Exchange. Stock and poultry were increased until a glut of foreign eggs began to oust the British variety. The country wanted cheap food as always and nothing was more unpopular than to suggest restriction of imports by taxation.

In 1927 partial rating relief was given and the grading of produce was introduced. We erroneously felt that, by producing Grade A stuff, better prices would accrue but as usual the public took the line that the cheapest was best whether home produced or not. Short and long term credits were made available for farmers. Money could more easily be borrowed but it was harder than ever to pay back. A farm sale is a sad occurence at any time but I went with my father to several sales caused by bankruptcy and these were even worse. Before the last war townsmen were wont to deplore farm subsidies but even the professional croakers must have been converted by the turn of events.

In 1932 a noble Viscount wrote: "The farmer is incapable of loyal voluntary co-operation and will sell the pass every-time". After the war, however, Lord Woolton summarized the nation's indebtedness to farmers, their men, wives and families plus the Women's Land Army, when he declared that, but for their efforts, we should have starved and lost the war.

Chapter 4

In the spring of 1929, after forty-four years as Rector of Hawstead, Leslie Mercer died whilst on holiday with his people at Sandling Place, Maidstone. Coincident with his death, a horse-drawn Church Army Caravan was in the parish. Two Church Army Officers were conducting a mission. In the spring of 1931 the caravan came again, and this time I was very impressed. That same summer I attended an evangelistic week-end at Church Army headquarters near Marble Arch and met that remarkable man, Prebendary Wilson Carlile for the first time. Undergraduates and miners were among the mixed bag of guests we joined in the services at Speaker's Corner in Hyde Park. I was really shaken. Each one of us had to give 'witness' as to what God meant to us. I felt a call then and there to full-time service.

By coincidence, a few weeks afterwards Prebendary Carlile conducted one of his famous "World Call" services in St. Mary's Church, Bury St. Edmunds and I renewed personal contact with him. The following winter saw me helping at services in St. Mary's Mission Hall under a Church Army veteran, Captain F. Price. I was thankful for that chance as there was little encouragement from the clergy, and I would have given anything to have read a lesson in a village church.

March 1932 saw me taking a big step. I joined the Church Army. Prior to so doing I 'burned my boats' by selling up the few pigs and poultry which I had kept on an acre of land owned by Mrs. Booth. I had paid a shilling a year rent, called a Peppercorn rent in the old days. Here I had also cultivated

Author with the Church Army caravan, 1932

a garden and kept some prizewinning Chinchilla rabbits. At the Church Army headquarters I was literally turned 'inside out' together with a bunch of probationers living a communal life under Spartan discipline.

The day began at 6 a.m. with a compulsory cold bath followed by household duties performed in absolute silence, broken by morning Chapel and followed by morning lectures. Slum visiting and band practice occupied the afternoons and each night found us in Hyde Park and "fishing" for congregations in Edgware Road. Almost the first person I invited told me to 'Go to Hell' and a crowd formed. It was a full fifteen minutes before I plucked up courage to ask another.

Hyde Park was a time of testing. It was all very fine to march out in Church Army uniform with a banner, singing "Onward Christian Soldiers" with thirty like-minded fellows. On these occasions we gave short talks interspersed by hymns and choruses. Often a gang of prostitutes would clamber on to our tiny platform and stroke our hair as we spoke! The big test came later when we went out with a chair, clambered on it and invited questions. On one evening I was asked twenty questions of which the following were typical: "Who made God?" "Where did Cain get his wife?" "Give a definition of a spirit", "Why does a God of love allow children to die from germs?". These were hectic days but a good training for Philip the farmer's boy.

I think perhaps Church Army training would be excellent preliminary canter for all clergy. There is, I am sure, an undeniable value in using testimony and making preaching personal. Three ways are open and Church Army contained exponents of all three; the first two being quite valueless. A man caught up as a Pharisee, thanking God he is not as other men: or, as an egotist who glories in the disclosure of his own baseness; or, in absolute sincerity because God has given him something, which for the life of him he can no longer keep to himself. In this case, as he bears witness to the change wrought in him, his neighbour may be helped and the angels will rejoice.

Unfortunately, before leaving headquarters for further training I had a recurrence of my throat and lung trouble. My first billet was at Newcastle-under-Lyme in the Potteries where I assisted a 'Parochial' Church Army Officer in charge of a mission church and band. That summer (1932), I went on a route march from Gloucester to Great Yarmouth and enjoyed it all. After a week-end at Gloucester (a cathedral city was chosen each year), fourteen columns of eight crusaders were dispersed to their various seaside destinations. We walked all the way and dragged a trek-cart, each man being allowed one suitcase and three blankets, plus a ground sheet. I was given the job of unofficial scribe and photographer to the party. For these summer crusades our dark grey uniforms were discarded in favour of officer's uniforms discarded from World War I.

It was a mass of packing and unpacking, introductions and farewells. We concentrated upon open-air services, informal church services and visiting and, of course, we never entered a parish without the incumbents' permission and fore knowledge. Sometimes we were fed collectively in village halls. Quite often, on arrival at a fresh parish at midday, we would be sent on another route march to get a meal! Our walking mileage was therefore quite considerable. We slept on the floors of village halls, schoolrooms and, in fine weather, on vicarage lawns. You see, when we joined Church Army, we were promised little else save board and lodging and on these occasions we appeared to be getting a darn sight more "board" than lodging!

At week-ends we were in larger places and were allowed to preach in churches. My very first pulpit was at Hampnett — a lovely Norman Church in rural Gloucester. Our route from Gloucester was via Northleach, Oxford, Luton, Newport (Essex), Halstead, Stowmarket and Bungay, and on July 27th we reached Yarmouth. We had taken seven weeks. There had been zig-zagging in order to cover parishes which had never received Crusaders before. Our actual marching mileage was three hundred, but with the intermediate walking this figure could be doubled. I had meals in eighty-three different houses and our organist played on thirty-seven church organs in seven counties.

After a month's mission on Yarmouth sands and a short leave at home, I spent the following winter on a horse-drawn Church Army caravan around Kings Lynn and Fakenham, Norfolk. On these missions we stayed fourteen days in the one parish holding weeknight Lantern Services. The big

The Church Army mission in progress on the sands at Gt. Yarmouth in 1932.

drawback here was really domestic. In those days caravan walls were thin and not insulated. Our heating was by a miniature coal-fired stove. The fire would be out in a couple of hours and next morning we were frozen. You see, it was a winter operation. We Church Army "tramps" had become "gipsies". I was particularly unlucky, being too long for the bunk, I had to sleep on the floor. We did our own meals and cleaning, but some parishes were quite lavish in their hospitality. We certainly found variety in Churchmanship and of course in Parsons. Whenever we were due to move to a fresh parish a farmer sent us a harnessed carthorse and we hitched up and departed.

I was recalled from the caravan to deputise for an ill Rector in the parishes of Stanningfield and Bradfield Combust. It was a coincidence that these were my father's home parishes as mentioned in my first chapter. What was even more strange was the fact that the Rector whom I helped, was farming his own Glebe and some of the very land which my forebears had farmed. In this latter connection I combined the parochial duties with farm-work!

During further training back at Church Army's London headquarters I became ill and spent some time in Middlesex Hospital. After this came a period in a poor district at Shepherd's Bush where one of my many jobs was selling 'Church Army Gazettes' in seven public houses every Saturday night. It was a sad blow to be 'invalided out' of the Church Army in 1933. The medical report said I was "medically unfit for aggressive evangelism and would always be subject to throat and lung trouble."

The Church Army found me a temporary post at Hartest, Suffolk again deputizing for a sick Rector on very familiar ground. I was in 'digs' at an Uncle's house — the family were "Brethren", but of course there was no discord. Local clergy were hostile towards myself filling such a gap and I found difficulty in getting exchanges in order that a priest could come and take a Communion Service sometimes. One of them explained that "His Squire objected to Lay Readers who were not Oxford or Cambridge men". Very grudgingly a Lay Reader's licence was granted me at this time.

In 1934 I went to Culford to work as full-time Lay Reader under the Rev. W. S. Andrew. Here were four amalgamated parishes: Culford, Culford Heath, Ingham and Timworth. With good lodgings and congenial work I was a happy man. At that time the Culford Hall Estate, belonging to Earl Cadogan, came under the hammer and involved six villages. Every cottage, in the end, was sold singly. At the five-day furniture sale at the Hall the State Coach made £28. It had been used by their Majesties Kings Edward VII and George V on their visits to the Cadogans for shooting, as this district was a famous game preserve and included some Breckland. The break-up of this large estate meant the loss of good jobs to a number of people.

Culford Heath was a vast tract of unspoiled countryside in those days. Plovers wheeled overhead answering the piercing cries and the whistle of the Curlew, a rather rare bird which nests here, could be heard. The rugged 'openness' was broken by belts of conifers with here and there an ancient earthwork — tumili, of which 'The Hill of Health' is an excellent example. The gipsy in George Borrow's, 'Lavengro' was responsible for the much quoted passage, "Life is sweet brother . . . there's a wind on the heath". Dwellers there would disagree. For them, 'wind on the heath' meant a sand storm and a farmer in the vicinity told me he was not sure sometimes in which parish his fields lay — it depended on the way the wind was blowing! Some of the houses I visited by tracks and bridle were in very remote areas. Paths gave rise to peculiar place names such as 'Sandy Barracks', 'Balloon Barn', 'Lands End Villa', 'John 'O' Groats' and 'New Zealand Cottages'.

When singing Psalm 104 I used to think of bobtailed rabbits

on Culford Heath. Now, however, Bible scholars tell us that the "conies" of the Bible were shapans — Choerogryllus, undoubtedly the Hyrax Syriacus. Anything but a rabbit! Nevertheless the old name persists in police courts where a man may still be prosecuted for trespassing in 'search of conies'.

A rabbit on a Culford farm was once seen making ineffectual attempts to mount some five foot netting. At last he mounted the back of a recumbent bullock. He was within thirty inches of the top so began to scratch the bullock who rose up in annoyance and the rabbit achieved his objective. It was also whilst at Culford that I heard of another version of 'Bull in a China Shop'. It happened at Fakenham, Norfolk when Queen Mary was actually in the shop. A bull, escaping from the cattle market, dispelled the old tradition by entering the shop, paid homage as a courtier to his Queen and left again without any damage.

It was at this time that I began to realise more and more that my true vocation lay in the Priesthood of the Anglican Church. I approached several clergy for advice, but received no encouragement. One or two said flatly that I hadn't a dog's chance. Personal appeal to two local Bishops was likewise disappointing. One told me to get back to pig-keeping as 'his gardener' had told him pigs were a paying proposition. I next wrote to a number of theological colleges but always received the reply that they could not accept me without a Bishop's nomination as I was twenty-seven years of age and had no university degree. I then wrote to most of the English Diocesan Bishops. Their replies were a heart-break. The gist of their letters conveyed that they were 'inundated with applicants and could only take graduates". The publication of their Ordination lists proved to me again and again how false these statements were. The crude truth of course was that I had nobody to 'pull the wires', yet the papers were full of stories of a big clergy shortage. I know that if I had not been sure that God was calling me I would there and then have given up hope.

At long last, after a wait of several months, my written application to the Bishop of Liverpool, Dr. Augustus David, was answered by Professor Charles Raven of Christ's College, Cambridge. He saw me in his rooms and I found him sympathetic and kindly. Eventually a letter arrived from Liverpool offering a sporting chance that I might be accepted after three or more years at St. Andrews, Whittlesford, Cambridge subject to my passing a General Ordination Examination.

With my own small savings augmented by help from friends (no public grant!) I entered St. Andrews in January 1936 and was there during the reign of three Kings — George V, Edward VIII and George VI.

I found the studies difficult and irksome yet it was good discipline. We lived a communal life and for some time I was responsible for cooking breakfast for the whole community on an Aga cooker. We also worked in the garden, in the parish and at Duxford aerodrome. I was now sharply confronted with 'Modernism' and a great disbelieving outlook on theological beliefs. I emerged convinced of the hopelessness of so much modern teaching and over forty years Ministry as a parson has not shaken my faith in this respect.

The Chapel at St. Andrews, Whittlesford was in daily use by staff and students and we used 'Songs of Praise'. Whilst I fully appreciate the inclusion of some very fine hymns which had previously been neglected, this compilation, by excluding some fine hymns and mutilating others, will never supersede such a book as 'Ancient & Modern' (revised). At least the compilers of the latter cannot be accused of 'watering down' the Christian faith. My vacations were spent working on Bryers Farm and doing what reading I could in the evenings, whilst on Sundays I continued working in many parishes as a Diocesan Lay Reader.

At length after a stormy passage, examinations were completed and I received my 'Deacon's Papers'. Life at St. Andrews and contact with University had opened my eyes to the vast amount of wire pulling which goes on and by which men sometimes are literally pushed into Holy Orders. In other words, their training was like a donkey's gallop — soon over. However, to write thus could seem to be sour grapes but truth needs to be stated from time to time. I had my thirtieth birthday at St. Andrews, Whittlesford and eight days later, on June 12th, 1938, I was ordained deacon in Liverpool Cathedral. Had it been possible for my parents to be present in that vast and comparatively modern place my joy would have been complete. As it was, my sister Molly and brother Maurice were there, so were my mother's cousin from Brixton and Annie Walker, an old family friend for whose prayers and practical sympathy I had so long been grateful. The service was wonderful and with it came a sense of relief that no man could ever again forbid my Ministry.

Chapter 5

I began my curacy immediately in the huge dockland parish of St. Mary, Bootle with the Rev. Fred Lloyd (later to be Canon) who only died in 1978. He was a grand little man; unconventional, sincere and a glutton for work. It was the parish church of Bootle and although uninteresting architecturally and with grotesque interior ornamentation it stood for a witness to a faith which could rise above the sordid in those mean streets of dockland. The visiting was hard, pathetic and amusing at times. Here people were subconsciously feeling the call of the countryside, the graveyard, the pot-plants, window-boxes and garden plots (if there was one). All testified to the revolt of a life completely divorced from nature.

I recall a conversation with a man at a small flower-show there. He had long been unemployed and he told me that but for his allotment he would long since have been driven mad or rotten. Masses of flowers appeared as if by magic into five of the big hospitals where I visited. These helped men and women to forget if only for a time, the suffering, the lust, the cruelty and the shams and ugliness of life. It must help those whose lot is cast amid brick and concrete to grasp something of the mystery of life out of death, the re-enacted parable of the changing seasons and the annual miracle of seed time and harvest.

Bootle as I knew it, held the highest birth-rate record for all England, and a walk round the streets would only confirm one's belief in the figures! There was a big Irish population

St. Mary's School, Bootle. The author with his vicar and Church Army sister ran an unofficial school in the parish for the benefit of children who did not evacuate, 1940.

both Roman Catholic and Protestant and I have seen frequent clashes between the Roman Catholics and Orangemen, each seeking to wreck the other's procession. I have also seen women fighting like cats and dogs in the streets.

It was not uncommon, even then for crowds to turn hostile to the police, and broken heads were commonly admitted into Bootle General Hospital where we did the Chaplaincy.

I had many Baptisms and funerals. The latter often with a horse-drawn hearse and the horses bedecked with black ribbons. There were no cremations then in so far as I was concerned. I came across an unusual (to me) expression one day which apparently was quite usual in the district. Relatives were speaking of the departed; "anyhow, sir, we buried him with ham". I found this referred to the knife and fork tea which followed the service! A local firm of undertakers also surprised me with their custom of presenting the local clergy with a handsome box of cigarettes, the box being in the form of a model coffin. The gift didn't apply to curates and, anyway, I was a non-smoker. A huge building near to the church was used by Littlewood's pools and over a thousand girls were employed there. At that time the Liverpool clergy were denouncing pools in no uncertain terms, but Fred Lloyd, my Vicar, saw that they had come to stay and so we began lunch hour services for the girls and these were greatly appreciated. The Lad's Club and the Church Lads Brigade were happy spheres and every week we showed films to four hundred children, my Vicar being a keen supporter of the cinema. Many of the kiddies were barefoot and dirty; quite small children would bring baby brothers or sisters wrapped in shawls. The atmosphere of the Church Hall was putrid but everyone seemed gloriously happy.

Living near to Aintree I twice saw the Grand National. The second year I saw two horses receive their death wounds at those wicked jumps and I have condemned that type of race ever since. I also cycled up a time or two to see Everton and Liverpool play soccer but was more at home watching our local schools play on Saturday mornings. Unfortunately my health began to suffer and throat and chest trouble led to a bout in hospital just before my Ordination to the Priesthood.

In September 1939 I went with my sister, her friend and future husband on a tour of Scotland, where we climbed Ben Nevis. The country was at war before I returned to Bootle. I subsequently returned home to conduct my brother's wedding at Hawstead. He had taken over Bryers Farm in the Spring of 1939 and my parents had removed to New House which they re-named The Beeches. This marked the retirement of my father from farming, before which he had invested in a tractor, an oil-engine and a Mill so that the farm, for its size, was well equipped. My father's counsel to my brother, and indeed to all of us, was "let your eye be your guide, and your money the last thing you part with".

After my hospital bout I changed from my most unfortunate digs to a bed-sitting room where I lived a somewhat hermit-like life and had my mid-day meals at a local hotel for eighteen pence — that sort of meal today would be worth at least £2 or more. For half-a-crown I could hire a cob and ride on the sands at Waterloo by River Mersey for one whole hour.

The following January found me ill again in Bootle General Hospital. Ever a convinced bachelor I now seriously thought

60

about marriage. Amy Newton from Southport was my
night nurse (afterwards a night sister) and we were good
friends before my eight weeks were up. It was at this time
that the medical authorities declared I must return to the
East Anglian climate. It was a wrench leaving Bootle at the
end of June because I had been happy there and so lucky in
my Vicar. How important is a man's first curacy! One of
my treasured possessions is the Private Communion set
which was among my parting gifts from the Parish. The
Church was subsequently destroyed during the German
bombardment of the docks on Merseyside.

During the break after Liverpool, I had one hectic week!
Throwing aside my customary caution I became engaged to
be married, bought a secondhand Ford eight for £36. 10s.
and also a typewriter.

The author's engagement gathering. He is seen here with parents, brother and sister-in-law, 1940.

In July 1940 I began a curacy in the magnificent Parish
Church of Saffron Walden, Essex. It was like being Precentor
at a Cathedral and I had secured the post through a *Church
Times* advertisement. After six months in excellent digs,

Saffron Walden Parish Church where the author spent four years as Curate.

I was offered the senior curacy and the house which went with it. The cleaning, decorating and furnishing dug a hole into my savings and my stipend was £200 a year! In 1941 we were married in the parish Church by the Vicar, Doctor Leonard Hughes. I joined the National Fire Service, began a Company of the Church Lad's Brigade and regard this and the Army Cadet Force as the finest organizations for the youth of the Church. We soon had over 70 boys and a drum and bugle

The Church Lad's Brigade formed by the author at Saffron Walden in 1940.

band going. There was a flourishing Church Sports Club and in the local Amateur Dramatic Club I became Tallent in Emlyn Williams play, "The Late Christopher Bean".

In the summer of 1942 I started a Young Farmers Club in Saffron Walden. There were very few in all England then and I became its first leader. It was not the social sporting venture club which is so often the case in 1980, but although we had our lectures and farm visits we took over two acres for cultivation and stock-raising on a co-operative basis and did our own work.

What a lovely place is Saffron Walden; absolutely unspoiled and full of genuine charm and beauty. I soon made the acquaintance of Alfred Tressider Sheppard — a poet of no mean ability whose brother was then Provost of Kings College, Cambridge. The whole town was one parish and we did the Chaplaincies at the 'Union', which I re-named 'St. James Hospital', and the Ancient Endowed Almshouses.

In addition, we had charge of Sewards End and Little Walden; the latter small church being my own particular charge. I was again fortunate in my Vicar, a scholar and Doctor of Divinity who had a long innings there in spite of extreme deafness. Unwavering in principle, resolute yet kindly, Leonard Hughes was an extraordinary man and not many parsons shared his distinction of once refusing a Canonry.

I attended the Diamond Jubilee meetings of the Church Army in May 1942 and shall not easily forget the frail but vital figure of dear old Prebendary Carlile, then ninety-five, as he addressed the meeting that day with his sister at his side. He warned us not to become too respectable but to continue to go for the worst. After the meeting I had a word and a hand shake from him. I am glad to have known a man who accomplished so very much and who enabled Laymen (and women) in their hundreds to find a niche within the Church. Before that year ended I attended his funeral in St. Paul's Cathedral which was packed—royalty, professions, Church, civic life and the Services were all there to pay tribute to his life and work. Yet when he began, sixty years earlier, he had faced opposition everywhere, both without and within the Church.

On January 8th 1942 a son was born to us, John Newton

we called him, and he was badly wanted. I have always loved children but until his birth babies, in my eyes, were just babies. They either screamed, wetted or else were very good at their Baptisms — now they seemed different. I am sorry for the childless couple when it is not their own fault, but when it is, I feel just as sad. Divorce courts today are filled with those who plunged into marriage to have a good time and many couples who found their so called "freedom" were often, if they tell the truth, just pining for the servitude of a family.

Parenthood imposes ties, self-sacrifice, menial work and so on but above all there is a transcendent joy. The father who feels a tiny hand placed in his own, and the mother who can gaze into the eyes of a child she herself has borne, will know they have a treasure which the world could never supply.

In October 1942, I took my sister's wedding at Hawstead. She married Stanley Peck, also a teacher, and subsequently their son, James, joined the profession.

I had a bout of pneumonia during 1943 but picked up so well afterwards that I thought seriously again of offering myself to the Army. Earlier, the Bishop had said that I couldn't be spared and yet he was one of the many who had refused me altogether some years previously. It was no quick decision. Months of prayer and thought had prompted it and now, looking back, I know I was right to go ahead.

The "intake" course at Tidworth was a happy experience although I very nearly passed-out while running at the double, wearing a gas mask. Our Commandant, Frank Woods, was a Bishop's son and afterwards he, too, became a Bishop. He was a great leader and was admirably supported by John Arthur, one time Vicar of Castle Rising who had served in the R.F.C. in the first war and, in the last war, had laid aside his dog collar for an Artillery Commission. He then resumed Chaplain's rank to help train us.

The crowded course finished and I was sent for a grim three weeks at Cusworth Hall district Headquarters near Doncaster. I was then posted to Hull Garrison from which I covered static units of the East Riding. Transport was a major problem, but I soon acquired a utility truck with a peculiar history. It had been loaned to a Padre on the coast

64

and the unit had moved on and left him with it. One day he drove it to a Fort in the Humber at low tide and it became submerged for 24 hours. After recovery some backroom lads in workshops at Hull removed the ravages of salt-water and she was "rested". I inherited the vehicle and a pack of trouble and drove it often when I should not have done.

My duties took me to Spurn Point, the bleak isolated end of the Holderness and where the first "mixed" battery of Artillery — men and women, was formed. Here for a time I found a musical, artistic, popular Major Beecher-Stowe in charge of a Coast Artillery Battery, and his unusual surname led me to discover that he was the great nephew of Harriett Beecher-Stowe, the hymn writer and author of *Uncle Tom's Cabin.*

Christine Mary was born to us in July 1944. These were anxious days, for East Anglia was still very subject to enemy action and my wife and John were on their own. I could

Philip Wright with his wife and children in June 1945 whilst on Army leave.

feel for the men in the services and am glad that I voluntarily shared a spartan life and the separation which it brought. Well-meaning folk criticise the Royal Army Chaplain's Department for giving the Padre a rank which involves a salute. The "pips" never once prevented me contacting the men when and how I liked. The wearing of battle dress gave me free access to mess room and canteen. From the very outset I made the salute a friendly greeting between comrades with a civil "Good morning". I never found an objector, and in my turn I, too, got quite a kick out of saluting all higher ranks than my own captaincy. Formal and informal Church Parades and Padre's hours played a big part in my Army career. Sometimes I 'borrowed' a Church, often I used a canteen or mess room; even Nissen huts became Churches by covering a table with an army blanket or Union Jack. On these I set out my oak cross and candlesticks, to provide a focal point for the lads' vision. Padre's hours were grand opportunities for Christian teaching and discussion. I tried to avoid politics and secondary issues but many were the problems I attempted to handle. Compassionate leave and matrimonial troubles were prominent.

My next posting was to Sheffield where, in "Steel City" I was attached to an R.A.S.C. driver — training Battalion, and I covered, in addition, the army patients in nine hospitals and four static units. I had a friendly mess with one of the best commanding officers in Colonel Barker-Simpson. He was forthright, jovial, human, and the son of a former Suffolk Parson. It was here that my health cracked twice more and I spent some time in Wharncliffe Hospital, part of which was entirely military. In the Autumn of 1945 I was invalided out and, after certain Ecclesiastical promises failed to be honoured, I was glad to accept Lord Braybrooke's offer of Littlebury, near Saffron Walden. I also combined this with the position of Army Welfare Officer for North West Essex until four years later when Army units took over their own Welfare. I also accepted a commission in the Army Cadet Force which ran concurrently and which I eventually held for no less than twenty-eight years.

Chapter 6

Littlebury proved a happy sphere, and being only two miles from Saffron Walden we had lots of friends in the district. The Church is a gem. It has Norman work, a richly carved font case, two fine porches and some nice brasses; it is also the burial place of members of the Braybrooke family of Audley End. There is a daughter Church at Littlebury Green which I served and I took on the Chaplaincy at Saffron Walden Union — St. James Hospital.

I was kept quite busy with my Army Welfare work for the first four years as well as running my own Platoon of Army Cadets and later commanding the Company at Saffron Walden and from thence second in command to the 5th Essex Cadet Regiment. We had open air services at Rogationtide and annual fetes at the vicarage when I had the audacity to give Punch and Judy shows and ventriloquist performances. The latter was inspired by a gift from "Big Bill" Campbell, the western entertainer, who lived opposite the vicarage, of a ventriloquist doll in his own likeness. I had the sad task of conducting the funeral of his little five-year old son Bobby and Bill's own funeral later in 1952 when he collapsed on the stage at Ipswich Hippodrome. An impetuous, likeable chap, he once bought a race horse at Liverpool during Aintree week and telephoned requesting me to meet it at Audley End Station and lead it home on a dark night along the very busy A11 road. I stuck to the footpath as much as I could!

I was elected to serve on Saffron Walden Rural District Council in 1946, but found it embarrassing when a council house became vacant in the parish. Eleven people wanted it but only one could have it and the rest blamed the Vicar! A year later my little book of reminiscences and poetry was published under the title *'Plowshare & Pulpit',* to be followed by a book of sermonettes, *'Padre Calling'.*

For many years I wrote a monthly article in the *'Cadet Journal'* called "The Padre says . . . " This was followed in 1950 by a booklet to aid lads being conscripted for National Service, under the title *'Joining Up'* and this was well-received.

In 1948 I helped stage the first ever Army Cadet Tattoo held at Dunmow and by that time I had formed a team of handbell ringers who entertained.

I was, for a time, Honary Secretary to Saffron Walden Horse Show and in 1949, when the Essex County Show came to Audley End Park, I became their press steward and in addition stewarded the Long Service awards given to men who had put in forty, fifty, and even sixty odd years either with the same boss or on the same farm. I did this job for the next thirty years without a break only to hand it over to my son John, in 1978. Throughout my career as officer and Padre to the Army Cadets of Essex, I put in twenty-six annual camps and these were truly great occasions — a real break and no holiday, but they became better value than a holiday could ever have been. I was not a restful spirit in those days.

My father passed on in August 1949 to be followed three years later by his sister Ada, our organist auntie.

I received a tremendous and pleasant shock in January 1954 when I was awarded a Military M.B.E. for services to the Army Cadet Force. Amy kindly allowed the two youngsters to attend the Investiture — only two persons were allowed. John was then twelve and Christine nine years of age. Since then, however, we have been four times to the Palace. On the first occasion Amy and I were guests when the representatives of all the Cadet Units in Britain marched past to be reviewed by Her Majesty and Prince Philip. The other three occasions were Palace Garden Parties.

We enjoyed our days at Littlebury but we laid to rest the body of our baby boy Paul Christopher, born to us in August 1949, after a very short life. The house was enormous and not modernized. We had eighteen rooms and an acre of garden which I tried to cope alone for the first few years.

The one room in the house which could be warmed was the oak-beamed ceilinged kitchen with its black-leaded kitchener. One hundred years previously, one of my predecessors had a family of nine and added a wing to a very ancient house.

There was a row of bells marked: Blue Room, Day Nursery, etc., but the days of domestic servants were long since gone, and so we sometimes rang them for fun and answered them ourselves. I would occasionally be invited to rabbit and hare shoots, and was sometimes able to bag a pheasant on my own domain. The late Robert Beck and "Lad" Engelmann both loaned me a horse when the Puckeridge Fox Hounds met locally, and I saw a good deal of the countryside from a different viewpoint than that afforded by the normal road-ways.

I always believed in an open Church and sometimes a tramp would turn up at breakfast and thank me for the night's doss in one of the pews! We did, however, once lose a sanctuary carpet and on the back of the replacement carpet I painted in large letters "Stolen from Littlebury Church". This one was never taken! We did, however, have the lead taken from the south aisle roof one night in December 1949 and had to replace it with copper. Such is the moral state of the world that I believe passing lorry drivers must have seen what was going on and never bothered to report it. The village school was just opposite the vicarage and both John and Christine began their schooling there. I took assembly once a week and then the top class for "Scripture lesson". This is a privilege of the utmost value which I have known some Clergy to shun or allow to slip from them. By the time we had left Littlebury, John had won a place at Newport Grammar School.

In 1950 we exchanged for two weeks with the then Vicar of Walton-on-the-Naze and among the highlights of that fortnight was being privileged to take the choir out for the Annual Lifeboat Service at which I preached from a rowing boat. We have such happy memories too, of nativity plays and carol services at Littlebury and, of course, harvest festivals. When Parson Hawker of Morwenstow summoned his Cornish parishioners to a harvest thanksgiving in 1843 the idea soon spread and commonly drew the largest congregations in town and country. Some cranks regret this fact and point out that the harvest festival has no ecclesiastical authority. Yet the desire to return thanks for bodily food is normal. Even your dog wags his tail when you feed him. To my mind no other occasion serves so well to link work with worship and thus to break down that barrier which sometimes appears to stand between religion and everyday life. Before I left the Army, under the title *'Our Daily Bread'* I produced a form of service for farm occasions which was published by Epworth Press and it is still going strong.

In 1953 after a long spell of painful physio-therapy on my spine which only made me worse, I was put into plaster and with splints and traction I spent several weeks in very hot summer weather in Addenbrooke's Hospital, Cambridge. I was conducting seven services on most Sundays as, soon after going to Littlebury, I also became Chaplain at St. James's Hospital, Saffron Walden.

My ten years at Littlebury terminated in 1954 when unexpectedly, and again quite unsought, I was offered the Benefice of St. Paul, Woodford Bridge, the last 'village' before Greater London. The Patron was Christopher Wansey, then Rector of Woodford, sometimes controversial but a delightful, dedicated parson of integrity. I thanked him (and I thanked God for him) and accepted.

Bishop Hugh Gough inducted me on All Saints Day that year, and on December 10th my former Vicar at Saffron Walden, Leonard Hughes, passed on at the age of 86. Woodford Bridge Church is built of Kentish ragstone and stands on a small green near a pond. It is Victorian and one of my first jobs was to get the brown and green interior walls lightened and to get the flaking outside walls treated. We had a smaller vicarage which had not been purpose built for the job. We had to have an auction of surplus furniture before moving there from Littlebury. To save petrol on my Ford Prefect I also rode a motor-bike for hospital visiting etc. around the area. John had transferred to Buckhurst Hill County High School and Christine to Roding Lane School followed by some years at Gowan Lea. At Littlebury we had to share with a Deanery Magazine but now I had my own Parish Magazine. As always I tried to express myself with candour and this sometimes led to press interest in wider circles.

On removal to Woodford Bridge I had to give up my

Cadet force command but remained as Senior Chaplain and Public Relations Officer until my official retirement in 1974 when I was sixty-six. I had received my ACF Long Service Medal in 1958 and a bar to the same ten years later.

By this time I had added considerably to my collection of farm bygones now crowded into a sectional hut at the vicarage. I donated many larger items to museums and other collectors. More by accident than anything I became involved in a revival of traction-engines and steam rollers. In the past they had meant periods of stress and hard dirty work when they brought the drum and elevator to Bryers Farm for threshing. In those far-off days I never dreamed I would be chasing the countryside to see these gentle giants racing and playing musical chairs.

The author with a veteran engine owner, Charles Bartrupt.

With the Queen Mother at the 1961 Essex Show presenting award to Long Service Farm Workers.

Philip Wright and his wife, Amy, pictured with H.M. The Queen at The Essex Show, 1978. Also in the photograph is the author's son, John.

the traction-engine world experienced some years earlier. A large number of articles, photographs and sketches had been published under my name by this time and I was also contributing regular farm columns in *West Essex Gazette* and *Essex Countryside*. My keenness for a close-up picture gave me a close shave and spectators a bit of a thrill on 3rd June 1964. This happened in the Grand Ring at the Suffolk Show when Colin Newlove was riding 'William' the Bull, which he had trained to jump like a horse including through a ring of fire. On this one occasion, however, instead of jumping the wall he went for me and gave me a jostling. Fortunately, I received nothing worse than very sore ribs. I think it must have been my coloured Army Chaplain's hatband which upset him — it always surmounts the straw-boaters which I wear in summer.

Unlike many clergy I never took a long holiday. I preferred odd days to visit shows and sales or to watch Essex County Cricket. However, in April 1963 Amy and I embarked on a journey of a life time. We visited the Holy Land by sea and overland route with Inter Church Travel. The Bible came alive again in a remarkable manner and it was an experience for which I shall never cease to be thankful. An anonymous member of the congregation helped to make it financially possible, and it helped me to recover from two operations in Whipps Cross Hospital.

A year later a suggestion I made to the Essex County Army Cadet Committee was put into effect and in May 1963 I helped to take a hundred Essex Cadets to Belgium. Amy, my wife, came with us as nursing sister and the object of the tour was training, goodwill and sightseeing. The weather was cold but the boys kept in good heart. Our barracks at Ghent was specially opened up but no heat was available. Coach visits were paid to Brussels, Waterloo, The Menin Gate, Ypres and Hill Sixty where some World War I trenches are preserved. The Belgians were delighted to see British Army uniforms once again.

After nearly eleven years in this tough but happy parish, the Bishop asked New College Oxford, the Patrons, to offer me the Benefice of St. Michael's, Roxwell, just out of Chelmsford. I said goodbye with very mixed feelings to a good choir, congregation and a splendid band of Church workers.

Chapter 7

Roxwell is an historic and rather lovely parish, with an area of seven and a half square miles and an attractive village street with Church, school and Memorial Hall within a stone's throw. Here lived Francis Quarles who, but for having clashed with Shakespeare, might have been better known. However, Horace Walpole complained that "Milton was forced to wait till the world had done admiring Quarles". He was born in Romford in 1592 and came much later to live at Newland Hall, which with many other charming houses and farmsteads still stands to this day. Four of Quarle's eighteen children were Baptized in the church and the Registers date from 1552. The poet's family had associations with the Stuart Court and Francis was an ardent pamphleteer defender of the King, at the same time possessing a Puritan outlook. Here is a specimen:

"My Soul, sit thou a patient looker-on,
Judge not the play before the play is done.
Her plot hath many changes: every day,
speaks a new scene: the last act crowns the play."

I am very fond of another of his short poems, because it could so easily have been written in 1980. It runs thus:

"Our God and soldiers we alike adore;
When at the brink of danger not before.
After deliverance both alike requited.
God is forgotten and our soldiers slighted."

Saving petrol at Roxwell Vicarage. The author and his wife with 'Jolly' and the governess cart.

Roxwell Church was built in the thirteenth and fourteenth centuries and has had some changes. In the nineteenth century restoration, the tracery from some of the old damaged windows was embedded in the roadside wall of the Church-yard. Soon after going there I brought up-to-date a huge burial board on which are inscribed the names of generations of folk buried there. I left it up to date when I retired in 1978.

The Bell was still chimed at the death of a parishioner,

and on Sundays, at 10 a.m. to remind parishioners they had
one hour to prepare for Church and at 6 p.m. again telling
them they had but thirty minutes before Evensong. This
custom went back hundreds of years. I had a prominent
board at the west end worded thus:

IMPORTANT
1. Visitors are never given the cold shoulder.
2. Services are never long.
3. Sermons are short and not read from a book.
4. The Church dates from the 13th Century, is full
   of interest but is not just a museum — some of us
   use it for worship.
5. You need God and God needs you.

In the parish is Skreen's Park, site of a mansion demolished
in 1924. It was the family seat of the Bramston's, one of
whom was Lord Chief Justice in the reign of Charles I.
Skreen's Park is now the Scout and Guide official county
camp site and I regularly welcomed hundreds to our services
in the course of a year. I also led assembly once a week at
the school and then took the top class for the first hour for
'Scripture'.

Author at a Meet of The Essex Hunt at Good Easter.

I had some splendid Church workers at Roxwell and the parish teemed with activities for young and old. We also had a beautiful modern vicarage which was a delight. Here too, I was able to regain possession of an adjoining field which I personally grassed down by broadcasting grass-seed, thereby making a good meadow in which I kept 'Job' the donkey and some aged horses belonging to the Ada Cole Memorial Stables at Nazeing. Subsequently I bought my own seven-year-old Chestnut Cob, 'Topper' at a Chelmsford horse sale and rode him regularly. I drove him in an Irish built trap which was nearly as old as me. I also rode him to hounds when they met locally. 'Job' also pulled a little donkey-cart and gave untold pleasure to local children. Our Labrador, 'Shane', used to ride on his back perfectly happily.

Having been a Steward at the Essex Show from 1948-1978, I suggested that at Diocesan level, we should try to have an annual worthy display there. We began to talk about it in 1956 and I went to see what was being done at the Royal Norfolk Show. I took some photographs of HM The Queen and Prince Philip inspecting the Norwich Diocesan stand. We invited builders and traders to help us in cash and in kind. When the itinerant Show became static in 1958 and anchored down at Great Leighs on permanent showground, we made our first venture under the title 'The Church and the Farming Year'. It was a wet show but I would like to quote the Essex County Standard which reported as follows: "Special mention must be made of the Essex Church who put on an imaginatively conceived, and beautifully executed stand; such artistry and imagination is not common". We had a small working committee chaired by the then Archdeacon of Southend (later to become Bishop W. N. Welch), Malcolm Carter, a farmer-artist, who was our chief inspirational designer and Harold Matthews, a tower of strength.

In 1959 with 'The Water of Life' we had as a centre piece, a high artificially built waterfall which took many days of hard work to produce. Jack Vyse used to select pictures and supporting photographs and each year we gave away thousands of specially printed brochures relevant to the topic and with a clear Christian message. We twice won the cup for the best "non-agricultural" stand and in 1960 we were runners-up. In 1961 we were honoured by a visit from The Queen Mother

The central feature at the 1954 Essex Show was this constant running waterfall made with canvas.

The author showing a group of children around the Church Stand at the 1963 Essex Show.

who expressed tremendous admiration for the stand which, under the title "The Bread of Life", had a harvest-field setting dominated by a huge working model windmill made for us by Felsted schoolboys.

We won the cup in 1962 with "The Good Shepherd' featuring live sheep and a quite remarkable figure of Our Lord which Malcolm Carter constructed from wire netting and Plaster of Paris. Our highly placed symbol of a huge cross surmounting a horse plough could be seen all over the showground. I am sad to record that since I retired from the Chairmanship in 1972, the plough has disappeared. In 1963 two huge hands held a constantly circling globe and the following year a swinging pendulum posed man between time and Eternity under the title, 'What am I?'' Other rather fine efforts were in 1965 when I persuaded Leslie Smith to set up his magnificent quarter-size model traction-engine and threshing drum which worked both days under steam for "The Sower" theme. In 1968 "The Meaning of the Cross" had my own donkey 'Job' in supporting role. Throughout the fifteen years I exhibited a number of my farm bygones relevant to the chosen themes. Before I made way for new blood in 1972 I was invited to take my slides and address a meeting of representatives of Church stand committees from all over Britain at the Royal Showground near Coventry. By the time I gave up, the animated Church stand on the Essex Showground had with its evangelistic appeal become a meeting-place for all comers. I recall a rather haughty lady leaving the stand and remarking that she couldn't for the life of her see why the Church should want to advertise. There was also a very small boy who, in response to my invitation to come in and look around, replied: "No. I already know about sin". But I like to think of the young farm worker and his wife; as they left the stand he turned to her and said: "It makes you *think* don't it?".

Whilst at Roxwell, the Guild of Agricultural Journalists honoured me by making me President for a year. Since then it has made me a Fellow and an Honorary Chaplain to the Guild for over a quarter of a century.

My job at Roxwell enabled me to continue my work within the Army Cadet Force both as an officer and as Senior Chaplain. However, in 1974 at the age of sixty-six

The author's farewell to Essex Army Cadets after 28 years!

having put in twenty-eight years service and attending twenty-six annual Camps, I felt it time to call it a day. I was duly "dined out" and given a splendid statuette of an Army Cadet. I look back with profound thankfulness for a wonderful experience. "Please sir. Can you teach me to sew a button on my trousers?" "Please sir. Will you write to my mum for me?" "Please sir. Can I go into the Church tent to say my prayers?" These are just three of the countless requests that have been my problem in these many years of annual camps. At one time Essex County took over a thousand Cadets to one annual camp. In those days the number was halved so that six hundred came the first week and then they made way for the rest. Homesickness was a problem occasionally but was often caused when the boys had too much free time. A busy unit was always a happy one. I always took a short epilogue in the camp cinema at the end of the last performance and often I was asked to go into huts or tents where the boys had missed epilogue through duties or manouveres. Always in camp there was one special parade service and also communion services.

Pacifists among Clergy and laity alike have criticised me for aligning myself to a military organisation. In my view, war in any form is evil and un-Christian; so too was Belsen and Dachau; so too are the present day evil concentration camps. When people say war accomplishes nothing, I cannot agree. History refutes this and when I see the names inscribed on war memorials, I realise that but for these the Gestapo (or something worse) would be in power here. It is precisely because of such sacrifices that people are still free to criticise and think differently from me.

The most glowing tribute our Lord ever paid to an individual was His great commendation of a Roman army captain (St. Mathew 8, verse 10). Surely it is better to teach lads to shoot straight at a target than to shoot at your windows! If the Army Cadet Force had not been a disciplined body I would never have touched it. The failing of so many youth clubs today and of so many church and school organisations, is soft leadership. We have spared the rod to our cost and the use of it is Scriptural and honest.

With the exception of Church choirs the Army Cadet Force is the oldest boy's organisation. Yes, we play at soldiers but with a sound purpose. It may surprise some readers to learn that one of the earliest Army Cadet Force pioneers was a woman, Miss Octavia Hill, also famed for her Sunday School work. In the 1960's she formed her Southwark Cadet Company in order to introduce London boys to the virtues of order, cleanliness, team-work and self-reliance. Now in the 1980s we try to carry out the same maxim for the betterment of the individual. Boys often find conditions of life which encourage neither honesty nor industry. Lack of religious belief deprives them of the moral balance which belonged to their grand-fathers, if not their fathers. The task of the Army Cadet Force, along with the home, the school and the Church, is to help a boy during the formative years of his life. No boy will join anything at all just because he wants to be improved! Therefore, without any apology we use military uniforms, discipline, terms and training. I was one of those who deplored the cessation of compulsory Church Parades when I was in the army, for there was more good than harm in them, and the excessive spit and polish of earlier days had been largely eliminated.

The author with Topper, a chestnut cob, in 1974.

If bodily fitness and mental training is considered vitally necessary, surely there is a case for compulsory moral teaching in which today we are all far too slipshod.

We assume that if a lad declares himself to be Roman Catholic or Church of England then he will sometimes want to worship within the way of his Church! A parade service is a great act of witness — a unit at prayer; and it makes it easier for a timid lad to be paraded with his mates.

Once during my army service a Sergeant Major was sorting out the lads for Church Parade. R.C. on the left, C. of E. on the right, other denominations, 'stand fast', he shouted. One man dropped out altogether, saying he was an atheist. He was sent to clean out the latrines. Next Sunday at the same procedure he was discovered among the C. of E. boys. "Oh no," said the Sergeant Major, 'you were an atheist last week." "I know I was,' replied he, 'but I've changed my religion. I didn't like the place of worship." One of the first things we teach recruits in the Services or in the Cadets is to do an 'about turn' and this reminds me of a young subaltern who was marching a platoon towards the cliff edge at Sandown, Isle of Wight. A visiting 'brass-hat' appeared and the young officer became tongue-tied and forgot his due order to 'about turn'. "For goodness sake shout something", yelled the Brigadier, "even if it's only goodbye." These lads in reality are walking towards the edge of a steep cliff and do not know it. They are battling with fears, toying with wickedness; and it is our job to remember the word of command, "Repent ye", which is the Church's 'about turn'.

In my long service with the Army Cadet Force I saw big changes. In earlier days officers were not paid for camps but the army was numerous in those early post-war years and did more for us in administration which we subsequently had to do for ourselves. For welfare funds we relied entirely upon our own fund-raising as do other youth services. Only accommodation, weapons and uniforms were free. Many such organisations begin within the Church. We had to break-in and bring in the Church. The majority of our boys were out of touch with things spiritual, a generation among whom many have never even been taught to pray. It was perhaps a compliment that a percentage of lads were sent to us by probation officers. Now we talk a lot about juvenile delinquency. It starts with examples from adults and if we can get lads to believe in God we shall begin to win the battle against Godless communism. This generation has for too long looked towards education, science, the press, the media and parliament for its redemption. The Salvation of young and old needs the old fashioned Gospel and somehow the Lord Christ must be put into their midst.

For eight years I wrote a monthly Padre's column in the *Cadet Journal* and also helped to formulate two syllabus courses which the War Office published for us. I also helped write *Cadets and the Church,* a booklet designed to help would-be Cadet Chaplains.

In July 1970 our only daughter, Christine, was married at Roxwell to David Beharrie from Fulham. We were delighted to have the then Bishop of Bradwell, W. Neville Welch, to take the service at which I helped after giving her away. They happily settled at Buckhurst Hill, not far from my old parish of Woodford Bridge.

The following year marked the golden jubilee of Chadacre, celebrated by a Thanksgiving service in Bury St. Edmunds Cathedral at which I was privileged to preach. My cathedral preachments have not been numerous but I previously preached at Bury St. Edmunds for a Harvest Festival, once at Ely and once at Chelmsford. I missed an invitation to preach at Sheffield Cathedral when in the Army because, when the time came, I was in a military hospital.

Daughter Christine with David on their wedding day.

After preaching farewell sermon at Roxwell.

The author receiving a £1,000 gift from parishioners of Roxwell on his retirement. Also in the picture are Mrs. Wright, his son and daughter and two grandchildren together with the two churchwardens.

Physically I found myself losing ground and three hospital bouts did not improve matters. One of these, in July 1976, was caused by a fall into a septic-tank when watching a village cricket match and which very soon necessitated an operation. I could so easily have lost a leg but the surgeons and nurses did a great job. Next I lost the sight of one eye which is not open to a cure.

We began serious house-hunting to discover that because of inflationary house values I was unable to purchase even the smallest of dwellings. I had, for life, carefully saved for such an eventuality only to find that I had not nearly enough. We therefore sought something a bit nearer to Christine and the grandchildren and were able to hire an ancient bungalow made from a stable. It is situated near to the famous little Church of Greensted, Nr. Ongar, a place linked with my former area near Bury St. Edmunds. This tiny Saxon edifice with its world famous wooden walls is the very place where the martyred King Edmund's body was deposited by the monks for one night on their way to St. Edmunds Bury as it was subsequently called.

Philip Wright Vicar of Roxwell, at Boyton Hall Farm selecting a pig which he afterwards auctioned publicly. He organised this in conjuntion with a fayre to raise money for extensive repairs to Roxwell Church.

After my farewell sermon and a wonderful send-off from Roxwell, which included a £1,000 cheque from parishioners, we went on a lap of honour round the village with my family and grandchildren in a dray drawn by two of Whitbreads magnificent Shire horses. We removed in November 1978 to Queen Anne Cottage, Greensted as tenants of the Diocese, having spent a lot of money making the place habitable.

We are now ten miles nearer to Christine and David and our two grandchildren — Russell, aged five and Jeanette, aged two. Our son, John, is now established as Property Manager

The author's grandchildren, Russell and Jeanette.

for the Firestone Tyre and Rubber Company. He has not yet married, has a flat in Kensington and comes home at weekends except when he is travelling abroad for the firm.

I have also been able to see a bit more County Cricket and to watch the success of the Essex team in winning championship status at last in the year 1979!

In retirement I hope to continue to be used in various parishes as a stop-gap as long as health and age allows. I also hope to worship from time to time with my friends in The Salvation Army until God calls me Home.

In my final chapter I am trying to express views and beliefs gleaned from my seventy-two years of great blessing from the good God.

Chapter 8

Many of us have lived long enough to realize that the real worth of higher and higher incomes does not, of itself, bring pure happiness but quite often the reverse. You have only to listen to those on the media whose lives seem appallingly empty of the things which really matter and their discontent seems so utterly obvious. Envy, apathy and disillusion is all there, and yet I have known hundreds of people who had less than their share of this world's goods and never grumbled. I have long felt that the Church has given some very bad leadership in this respect.

No so long ago a brand new Bishop in his enthronement address revealed in stark terms the deep cleavage within the Church as to her true terms of reference. He is reported as saying the three great issues of our day and St. Paul's day, are race, sex and class. Some of us believe the three great issues of today and St. Paul's day are sin, redemption and salvation. "Seek ye first the Kingdom of man through social justice" we are told by many of our present day Church leaders, and God will be found in the process. But this is a total inversion of Christ's original command. If our concern is primarily with man's earthly condition and not with his salvation, then we are turning the Gospel upside down. Jesus said: 'If any man would come after me let him deny himself and take up his cross and follow me.' He offered Himself alone not as an aid to human happiness but as 'The Way, The Truth and The Life'. To be sought for His own sake. The primary purpose of the Church is not to make men happy on earth but to get them to Heaven whatever subsidary purpose there may also be.

Our forefathers, in an age of settled standards, knew that the gulf between the way men behaved and the way they thought was regrettably wide, but they did not strive to persuade themselves or others that wrong was right. A Canon of Southwark called explicitly for a 'new moral code based on sympathy for the different needs of individuals who may 'need' to break all the ten commandments in turn'. Already this new subjective morality has come perilously near to the doctrine that whatever is done must be right.

A noble lord, apparently distressed at the number of irregular unions recently sought to remedy the situation by calling them all 'regular'. A Medical Officer for the Ministry of Education describes unchastity, in his view, as 'not unchaste'. These new moralists often accuse us who defend the conventional Christian code, of lacking in sympathy for those who sin. We do not lack sympathy and we know that we are bidden to beware of complacency and of unrighteousness knowing that we are all sinners. They, however, rest their case on the questionable assumption that restraint and moderation are the sworn enemies of happiness. Thus we find in the 'agony columns' of weekly woman's journals the columnists failing to give the distressed questioner the Christian standpoint and failing altogether to state that sex before marriage is wrong. Am I being utterly square and old fashioned if I declare that nobody should assume that it is normal and natural for a teenager, even schoolgirls, to automatically be given 'the Pill'.

A few years ago we had a Prebendary on the radio 'World at One' programme giving his liberal views upon the 'naturalness' of homosexuality, and declaring that there was no theological reason against this practice as a natural expression of affection. We need within the Churches the militancy of a Churchill, who in war time gave us all faith, hope and strategy.

Millions long to hear the authentic message of Christ's cure and answer to all kinds of sin. In more recent times we have learned of a "Gay Christian Movement", fully homosexual and supported by some Bishops and many Clergy.

What a travesty of the old word "gay" which meant light hearted joy.

At our Ordination we were solemnly charged to "banish and drive away all erroneous and strange doctrine". This is where the Church has let the side down, and so we now have a generation of youngsters, largely indisciplined, that has never met the challenge of adult authority. We are already reaping a bitter harvest from the "permissive" society, and I am becoming very tired of those adults who say we were all 'permissive' when we were young. If we had tried to get away with a quarter of the amount of deliberate anti-social behaviour as they do today we would have been challenged, punished and never again dared to attempt such things. Instead, today we have elderly dons and parsons aligning themselves with striking students and 'marching', i.e. slouching through the streets in one protest after another. Most of us thank God that indeed we were disciplined, punished and corrected. Most of us enjoyed our childhood and grew up unresentful of discipline, but a misfit minority were unhappy and it is they who urge youngsters to jump into bed with each other, to wear outrageous clothes, eliminate washing and haircuts, to take drugs and generally to abuse authority and attack the police. The TV and literature of the age has given them encouragement, and just note the ages of some leaders of student-rebels. They should have been at work years ago and away from universities. If students don't like their colleges or college rules then they should be told to get out and get a job or starve and make room for those ready to work; those who would give anything to be in their shoes.

It is an insult to people's intelligence to say they can no longer understand Elizabethan English. It is not the things in the Bible and Prayer Book which I *cannot* understand, which worry me. Instead it is the things which I *do* understand, i.e. the robust teaching of sin, salvation, repentence, forgiveness and the prospect of eternity. Therefore I shall go on addressing God as "Thou" and not "You". I also deplore the BBC radio morning service which has gone the other way to the great sorrow of millions of listeners.

I feel this very strongly when I consider the 1662 Service of Holy Communion and I think I ought to positively state how I view this service, for I have used no other. The first part of the service is of prayer and preparation in which our Lord speaks to us as He spoke to the disciples in the Upper Room. After the Lord's Prayer the collect for purity reminds us that only when the Holy Spirit inspires us can we worship God worthily. The Commandments (or their shortened form) tells of the Christian way of life and how we fall short of it. The collect is the Church's prayer for the actual work or the season it 'collects' and focuses in a few words the countless prayers of the people of God throughout the world. It is followed by the particular passage of Scripture known as the 'Epistle' and 'Gospel' for the day — i.e. The Word of God. The creed confirms our belief in the great truths of the Christian faith. The next part of the service concentrates on the bread and wine where our Lord takes emblems of the common things of life like eating and drinking and makes them symbols of His body and blood, broken and shed for us. We present ourselves as the only offering we can make in return. After the confession and pronouncement of His forgiveness comes that great act of worship wherein we join with Angels and Archangels and all the Company of Heaven, in blessing God for His gifts; above all the Redemption He offers.

Years ago we paid for our education or worked hard for scholarships and bursaries. Let us stand up to the noisy minority who would have us believe that anybody over forty is only fit for an old folk's home. This is our world (or rather God's world), and if some had not almost starved in the thirties or died in action in the forties they would not today be precisely where they are.

In other ways we are so very much indebted to the past and if this chapter seems to be a 'pot pourri' please forgive me. There is at the moment an insidious campaign for the eventual prohibition of the Book of Common Prayer and we who appreciate its completely 'Scriptural' basis should resist such a campaign. When the 'Act of Uniformity' was passed some clergy were imprisoned for refusing to use the Prayer Book. Now it seems likely that some may be pilloried for using it!

Contrary to the belief that archaic language is keeping folk from our churches, many feeling people (and I have talked to young and old about it) consider that today's tendency towards "exciting new forms of service" is derogatory to the worship of an omnipotent God. Noble language helps to draw mankind to the sublime; the inferior form presumes to drag God down to man. Here are the seeds of a very ancient heresy renewed. This is why I have resolutely kept to the old language in the face of an avalanche of clergy who seek to be 'with it' and who sometimes appear to be quite 'without it'. People have come from other parishes because of this very fact but the last thing I ever wanted was to become a 'sheep-stealer'. Even some of the modern translations appear to have watered-down the faith of our forefathers. I feel it would be out of place to discuss these here, but one appalling case is of the Lord's Prayer where the revisers, in place of 'Lead us not into temptation' render it: 'Do not put us to the test'. Surely life is always putting us to the test as God wills it.

The remainder of the service is praise and thanksgiving and I ask readers to read quietly the prayer of oblation and ask whether any bit of modern prose can match it? All of us join in the Gloria and the officiating Minister pronounces the Peace of God and Blessing.

In the past, when I instructed Confirmation candidates or Army personnel I always reminded them that this great service was being used in the loneliest Army hut, Mission Church, Parish Church and Cathedral, linking them in a wonderful way with the Church militant here on earth. The advent of Series two and three and the multitudinous variations these have brought, have made my words a nonsense. If only the reformers had addressed their efforts trying to revive the true purpose and calling of those who have felt called of God to serve within the ranks of the Church. It seems to me tragic that if I, for instance, hang up a picture or introduce an ornament, however suitable, inside a parish Church without a legal 'faculty' then I am in dire trouble with the authorities. If on the other hand I publicly deny articles of the Christian faith contained in the Bible and enshrined in the Creeds, nobody in authority bats an eyelid. Recently a parson, in his parish magazine, denied the Virgin birth of Jesus. Some have openly denied the after life.

A short time after I went to Roxwell I had to return to Woodford Chest Clinic for check-up and treatment at Hart's Hospital. Just outside the gate I met the local Vicar who was kind enough to say how much he missed my presence at the Clergy and Ministers' quarterly 'Fraternal'. He said that at their very last meeting a prominent Methodist Minister had openly stated he no longer believed in the Resurrection. My informant went on thus: "You know, Philip, I don't know which upset me most - the fact that he said this or the fact that the rest of the assembled brethren did not even comment."

I have consistently protested at Clergy Chapters and Deanery Synods and have been met with silence in the same way — stony silence!

In a small book I wrote in 1947 under the title *Ploughshare & Pulpit,* I wrote these words:

"There are many well-intentioned clerics who seek to win the world by linking up with a particular political party. Like myself, these men have seen the slums at close quarters and are reacting strongly. When, however, they link up subversive theories with Christianity, quoting apostolic days when they had 'all things common' they forget one thing. The all important ommission to my mind is just this: those early communists put the faith first and shared their goods afterwards. Modern communism is largely atheistic and we don't want to heap up inflammable material for less-worthy pagan hands to set fire to . . . "

We have lived long enough to see my prophecy fulfilled abroad and it can happen here if we allow it. People today yearn for spiritual bread even if they don't always know their need. Instead they are offered by the Church a political stone! The long cherished hope that there may be an escape route from the sorrows and vanities of this world is being brushed aside by the very one who should be assuring mankind that such a route does exist. Such clergy may think themselves progressive but they are merely adopting the assumptions which are fashionable today. They have chosen to concern themselves with a purely social Gospel concerned solely with the affairs of this world. Often on the media we hear pronouncements on religion by non-practising and non-professing Christians who have made their mark in the world of show-business and the like. They probably have forgotten when they last made contact with a decent Parson for instance.

To see them and hear them forcibly pronounce on the Church and its shortcomings is pathetic. They seem to be in the same position as would be the case if a cannibal was asked to preside at a vegetarian conference!

In spite of all our grumbles we have grounds for deep thankfulness to Almighty God. In an impatient world eager for the short cut, the fast road, the bigger pay-packet and the spectacular result, living now in retirement in rural Essex I feel that there is a more real environment awaiting anybody who is fed-up with the superficiality of much of 1980 living. We still have our world of lanes, woods, field, farms and of animals who often seem nicer and wiser than mankind. Even a stone's throw from the busiest motorway can be found the peace and quiet of the ages; a balanced scene presenting nature from birth, and maturity to the death and decay from which real life comes again. When I was at Woodford, the late Sir Alfred Munnings wrote me in appreciation of a small booklet I had written and illustrated. I hope I may be forgiven for quoting his letter . . .

"What an excellent work it is. You're a writer, you beat me to blazes in lesser space. I come up to town always by Stortford and Epping. What a forest! You could muse awhile in its groves gazing at its leafy floor . . . no place left quite like it. Your Woodford is rather a pernicious growth. Luckily the forest is left alone; so far and no further!

Go into its far beeches and shades and murmur a prayer for a lost and *crazy* world of fools . . . "

What a man he was and what an artist. I doubt whether anybody has painted horses as well as he. Some years later I took part in his funeral at St. James, Piccadilly.

Rapid changes are breaking in and I am sometimes scared of what could happen if the scientists and technicians are let loose on pastures and ploughland. If such are allowed to go forward without the immemorial wisdom of the country-side to guide them and without a thought for the Creator, then evil consequences follow for man and beast.

Thanksgiving has been the theme of many harvest sermons for generations but genuine farm folk will thank God for a lot of hard work finished. I have shown in this book that years ago it was a darn sight harder. I heard of a modern

Parson recently saying it is pointless bringing corn and fruit into Churches nowadays because everybody knows that you simply go to a shop or supermarket for food. How foolish! This is the great economic heresy of our age. What industrial mankind needs to be told is that food is not made in the supermarket. It has to be grown and the process takes a twelvemonth. Nobody can eat a pay-packet, however full.

Surely we do not need another war to teach us this lesson all over again? Politicians have talked a lot about standards of living needing to be higher, but often they merely mean that wages and dividends must go up, with better food, more drink and faster cars. Looking at this through a critical, but Christian, eye we can often see this becoming a very much lower standard of living when related to human contentment and real happiness. Meanwhile, work on the farm goes on unendingly and the stockmen are busy on behalf of everybody for 365 days of the year. I still maintain that farming is a way of life and that the modern word 'agribusiness' is revolting. The small working farmer is again under attack. Well, I was bred and born on one such farm as readers will know by this time! Money was tight and even if poverty was not a wholly good thing, we learned self-reliance and resourcefulness. We counted our blessings and thanked God for this. The Lord's Prayer puts it into the right perspective: 'Hallowed be Thy name, Thy Kingdom come, Thy will be done on earth as it is in Heaven', and then, and then only, dare we presume to ask for our daily bread.

God is still 'boss'. Nature often has the last word and even a crop-failure can lay foundations in character. We need to be grateful to the God who once in history took our nature upon Him and lived and died and rose again that we might live forever. This is a belief which outlasts time and will carry us into the presence of the great Lord of the Harvest Himself when our evening star appears. As the Prayer Book has it in the matchless words of a 'General Thanksgiving': '. . . We bless Thee for our creation, preservation, and all the blessings of this life, but above all for Thine inestimable love in the redemption of the world by Our Lord Jesus Christ - for the means of Grace and for the hope of Glory.'

The fact that the majority of super-markets now open every Good Friday is a clear indication at the popular level, as to the degree to which Good Friday, and the event it commemorates, are now denied any substantial significance in the minds of mankind. On the Cross, God made man, dies for the sins of the whole world and now it seems that the whole world could scarcely care less. Whose fault is this? It is easy for we Church people to lay the blame on the worldly secular society, and leave it at that: but the matter is not nearly so simple. If people obstinately refuse to accept the story of the Cross, then certainly they are to be blamed, but what if the Church has failed to preach this saving Gospel in season and out of season?

There has been this failure in many parts of the Church I am sure. Liturgical reformers, so keen to tickle the ear of modern man, have seemed determined to demote the Cross from its central place in the Church's worship. They have been followed by the writers of modern hymns and the mutilators of some of the old hymns too. Many of the world's best known preachers and teachers (including Bishops) have to my certain personal knowledge given scant attention to the Cross. Instead they have preferred to concentrate on those lesser aspects of the faith, which they think will make a more ready appeal to a generation which loves comfort and which is very complacent over religion. This same tendency is seen very clearly in the development of radio and television religious broadcasting from a clear-cut presentation of the faith to an apparent dissemination of doubt and uncertainty: from a truly Christian insistence on the absolute distinctiveness of Christianity to a pretence that there is little to choose between one religion and another, or between religion and none at all.

To hear many programmes under the title of 'religion' these days we would never dream that Christianity rests entirely on the centrality of the Cross and Resurrection of Jesus Christ as the one hope for the Salvation of the whole world; but it does you know!

The Cross always was a stumbling block to the sceptic, but it has always been the essence and the heart of the everlasting Gospel. St. Paul knew and declared it, so too did the Saints and so too did our more immediate forefathers. If one thing is quite certain it is that if the Cross, as the Key to eternal Salvation, was true for them, then it must equally be true in 1980. Reality and historic fact cannot be changed simply to suit the changing moods and fashions of men and women. There is an urgent and vital need for the Church to recover its true message and boldly declare it.

My final word must be concerned with the Resurrection. A small girl was recently asked what she knew about Easter? 'Nuffin', she replied. 'What's it in aid of, anyway?' Millions pay lip-service to Easter but know little more about it than that kiddie and a whole multitude couldn't care less. Those of us who really believe are a minority. I would have told that child that Easter is in aid of broken hearts, and homes. It is easy to dodge the great issues when life goes along easily and it is easy to laugh at the great truths. Generations are growing up when the only time they hear the word 'Christ' is when it is spoken as an oath, and on the TV screen. Our 'comics' feature a mock funeral with laughter and ridicule. The laughter dies down when they become personally involved, and stand by an open grave. Night brings darkness and a mother cries for her child, or a Darby is left without a Joan, or the other way round.

I know a sweet old lady of ninety whose husband, ninety-two, died at Christmas. She tells me how much she misses him and wishes they could have gone together. Easter is for these who have mourned but believed. How silly to tell them to have a few extra drinks, or that time will heal and enable them to forget. Why should anyone want to forget? Think of the poet's words: "He is not dead whose glorious mind lifts thine on high. To live in hearts we leave behind is not to die'. This couplet I recall from boyhood as inscribed on a memorial tablet just opposite to our family pew in Hawstead Church. The dead are awake according to the teachings of Jesus. It is only our foolishness that calls them dead. On the other hand, many are going about dead — dead to beauty, truth, goodness; dead to all but themselves. I am over seventy and my mind goes back to Bryers Farm, Hawstead where, in the wood, the flowers come annually — anemones, oxlips, bluebells and the daffodils which I planted in the 1920s. It reminds me that what God can do with flowers He can also do with you and me and those whom we love but see no longer. The Kingdom of Heaven is within us and we clergy are ordered to encourage folk to make a Will, to pay their debts, to visit the invalid and tell old so and so we no longer bear him, or her, malice. It is all contained in the Old Prayer Book in the Service for "Visitation of the sick".

A motorist was driving home one wet evening when he noticed several people waiting at a bus stop. He invited passengers. I did this once at Roxwell and got a dirty look from a bus inspector who took a poor view of my offer. Anyhow, this man collected a car-load and when passing the gates of a cemetery, a couple asked him to stop. He was surprised because it was late evening. The simple explanation was soon given. "Our home is the other side of the cemetery and we have a right of way through". This is the very heart of the Christian hope. 'I am the Resurrection and the Life,' saith the Lord. Our Home is the other side of the grave and by His Cross and Passion we have a right of way through.

The author photographed with Winston Churchill after having been introduced to the Great Man at Woodford Bridge in 1959.

The author was Mayor's Chaplain twice during his incumbency at Woodford Bridge and is seen at the Borough war memorial on Remembrance Day 1960.

The Queen Mother inspected the Essex Show Church stand in 1961.